ELVIS

A King Forever

ELVIS

A King Forever

Robert Gibson

with Sid Shaw

Elvisly Yours
P.O. Box 315
London NW10

Published by
Elvisly Yours
P.O. Box 315
London NW10

Copyright ©
Elvisly Yours Ltd

British Library Cataloguing in
Publication Data

Gibson, Robert
  Elvis: a king forever.
  1. Presley, Elvis – Portraits etc.
  2. Singers – United States –
  Portraits
  I. Title   II. Shaw, Sid
  784.5'0092'4   ML420.P96

ISBN 1-869-941-00-4 (Cased)
ISBN 1-869-941-102-2 (Paperback)

Typesetter Elements, London EC2

Reproduction Dot Gradations Ltd

First published 1985
Blandford Press

Reprinted 1986
Elvisly Yours

Reprinted 1987 (Twice)
Elvisly Yours

Printed and bound
in West Germany by Mohndruck

CONTENTS

INTRODUCTION 6

Chapter One
TUPELO 18

Elvis is born · The Gospel influence · The move to Texas
Elvis at school · His first guitar

Chapter Two
THE MOVE TO MEMPHIS 32

The family hits Memphis · Elvis the teenager
Enter Red West and George Klein · Elvis leaves school

Chapter Three
THE BEGINNING 46

Elvis's first recording · Enter Sam Phillips · *That's All Right Mama*
Elvis on radio · Elvis on the road · Enter Bob Neal
The Grand Ole Opry · Louisiana Hayride

Chapter Four
ELVIS MEETS THE COLONEL 58

Colonel Tom Parker · *Baby Let's Play House* · Elvis signed to RCA
The Dorsey Brothers Show · The controversy begins · Riots
Hollywood calls

Chapter Five
THE EARLY FILMS 72

The first screen test · *Love Me Tender* · *Jailhouse Rock*
Graceland · Elvis conquers Hollywood

Chapter Six
ELVIS IN THE ARMY 84

The Draft · Private Presley · *King Creole* · Gladys dies
Posting to Germany · Enter Charlie Hodge · Priscilla

Designed and produced by
Michael Balfour Ltd

Project co-ordinator
 Nicola Blackett-Ord
House editor
 Miren Lopategui
Production consultant
 Emma Bradford

Designed by
The Bloomsbury Group
2 Barbon Close, London WC1N 3JX

Artwork by
Charles Chambers Associates

Special thanks to The Elvisly Yours
Fan Club for editorial assistance and
supplying illustrations, and also to
The Elvis Presley Museum, USA.
The world's most extensive mail-
order catalogue is available from
Elvisly Yours Fan Club
P.O. Box 315
London NW10 England

INTRODUCTION

*The Country Star waited in the wings. Waited for the frenzy to subside. The audience had paid to see **him**. A country star. Not a country **boy** fresh from school doing his very first show before a paying public. But, as the hysterical kids chanted the boy's name, the Country Star must have wondered if they would even remember his, for he knew – just as the audience knew – that they had witnessed something special. Something **very** special. Whatever it was the kid had, he had it by the bushel. . . and the world by the balls.*

The country star shook his head slowly and, more out of admiration than out of envy, he shrugged, sighed deeply and said, "How can I follow that?"

No-one ever could. No-one ever will. For the rest of his life and now, even in death, that country boy has proved to be an impossible act to follow. He was to become the most desired, most envied, most emulated man of the century. And, perhaps, the most famous. So famous that he was known in every corner of the globe, by just his first name:

ELVIS.

Elvis Presley was more than the King of Rock 'n' Roll, more even than the Greatest Entertainer in the World. From the moment he set foot on stage at the Overton Park Shell, Memphis, Tennessee, in August 1954, for his first ever professional stage appearance, Elvis Presley was a revolution. He was to start a social upheaval that, in more ways than one, was to rock the world. The pounding rhythm, the shaking hips, the trembling legs and the quivering lips all set off shock waves that were to culminate in an earthquake that shook society to its core.

The social revolution that Elvis personified unchained young people from the restraints that had always shackled their parents, and sent long-established edifices of rectitude and respectability crashing to the ground – almost overnight age-old values and standards were uprooted and overthrown. It was also to establish a separate, quite different culture that belonged only to the young – and the young at heart. Like a twentieth-century Pied Piper, Elvis, with his music, lured the young away from the past and led them to another life, another world and another time.

John Lennon described it like this: "Before Elvis there was nothing. Without him there would be no Beatles."

"Elvis Presley made it possible for all of us to follow." *Buddy Holly*

The impact of his life was devastating. Just as devastating was his death. Wherever you were, it was the same. Whatever the time, it stood still. Whatever you were doing, you stopped. Whatever concerned you no longer seemed to matter. Elvis Presley was dead. It meant so much more than the death of a pop star, a rock idol. It was the death of an age. Youth promises immortality to each new generation. It is a promise that is always believed, but never kept.

To the post-war Presley generation it must have seemed a promise of substance. At long last Youth could have its fling. It was a time to be young, to have fun, to live, love and laugh. And there was the music. New, raw, vibrant, sexy. And there was Elvis Presley. New, raw, vibrant, sexy.

It must have seemed that it would never end, but it did – On 16 August 1977. It was on that day that a whole generation came face to face with mortality, for, if Death were no respecter of Legends and Kings, it could be no respecter of people.

Who – or what – was Elvis Presley? It is a question easy enough to pose, but impossible to answer. On a trip to Memphis with a party of devotees from the Elvisly Yours Fan Club of Great Britain, there were many personal tributes that helped to explain what made Elvis the phenomenon he was – and still is. A woman in her forties, with a grown-up family, said, "Elvis is everything to me. He is a dream lover, a brother, a friend. As the man of my dreams, my husband knows he will always take second place to Elvis. . . But strangely it is partly because of Elvis that I love my husband so much. He has always understood my obsession with Elvis and I love him for that. . . I know that I am lucky to have married such an understanding man. And of course, he knows I'm never really likely to run off with the milkman when I am so crazy about Elvis."

A young lad of 21 said that Elvis was many different things to him: "A lot of young people like the young Rock 'n' Roll Elvis. His older fans tend to go for the older Elvis. But me. . . I like Elvis, the gospel singer. . . If someone tells me they don't like Elvis, I tell them they cannot have listened to his music. He recorded so many different kinds of songs in so many different ways that it is impossible not to like at least something. Elvis has something for everyone."

OPPOSITE LEFT: *At home on his bike in Memphis.*

OPPOSITE RIGHT: *Candid early pose.*

TOP LEFT: *On the road with Scotty Moore.*

TOP RIGHT: *Backstage early candid shot.*

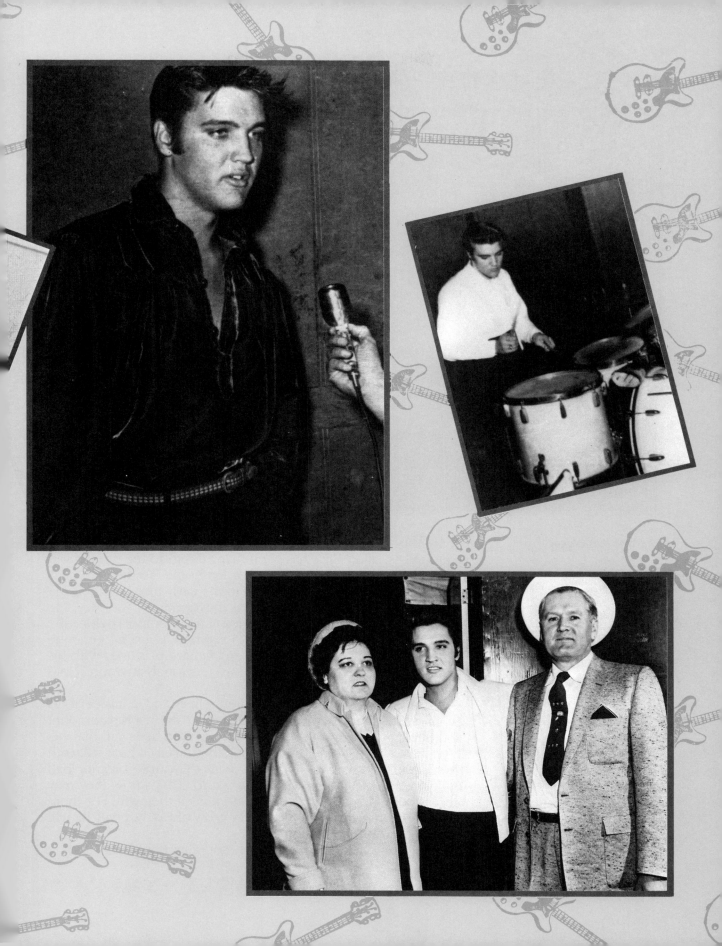

Elvis and the Colonel.

OPPOSITE LEFT:
G.I. Blues.

OPPOSITE RIGHT:
Mobbed by GI's in Germany.

Another lad, just 19, his hair dyed black and swept back like a young Elvis, said, "Elvis has been many things to me throughout my life. When I was a kid my father left home. To me then Elvis became a father. As I grew older, in my early teens, he became more of an older brother. Now he is my friend."

An old lady of 70, who had decided to see Memphis before she died of an incurable illness, said, "I see him as a son. Someone who is always there. The walls of my flat are plastered with his pictures. I turn on his music and I don't feel lonely anymore. He is a friend who never forsakes me."

Whatever part Elvis has played in the lives and fantasies of his fans over the years there is one role, a real role, that is paramount and permanent, that of friend, and it is a role he is still playing. Elvis fans never talk in the past tense; they talk as if he is still with them. And for them he *is* – it is as if a favourite brother had emigrated to the other side of the world. They know they may never see him again but they continue as if they will. For them Elvis is frozen in time – he will never grow old as they will; he will always stay the same.

Elvis has transcended mere superstardom. He has a

superhuman, supernatural hold upon his fans that will never be challenged by any other performer or personality – Elvis fans say they never feel the gnawing, empty loneliness so often experienced by others. He is always there, they say, a guide, a mentor, a comfort, a friend. He may have started as a sex symbol and may have remained one, but it is as all these things that he is remembered.

And, of course, as a revolution. Elvis may not have been the first drop of rain that fell on the mountain of mediocrity that was pop music pre-Presley, but he was certainly the torrent that swept much of it away. That the revolution would have happened without him cannot be disputed, but that it would have happened differently cannot be in doubt.

Was Elvis Presley really "unspeakably untalented", as one critic wrote in the late 1950s? Was he really just a "flash in the pan", as another claimed? Was he really just a puppet on a string pulled by a brilliant but exploitative manager? Perhaps the best answer to these questions is that today, more than 50 years after his birth, and nearly eight years after his death, I am sitting here writing about him.

Baby Lisa Marie with grandfather Vernon Presley.

RIGHT: *Another famous Pink Cadillac used as salad bar in the Heartbreak Hotel Restaurant (now closed) on Union St Memphis.*

OPPOSITE: *Famous photo taken with Muhammad Ali (cropped from picture*

Was he really the drug-crazed monster, the sex pervert and Mummy's boy that Albert Goldman in his savage book would have us believe? I suspect that Albert Goldman, confronted with the Bayeux Tapestry, would take out a pair of garden shears and none too delicately or skilfully, begin to take it apart, then, when finished, would smile, point triumphantly to the pile at his feet and declare: "There. . . I told you it was only sackcloth and thread."

Had Elvis been born to Kingship like some European princeling, trained at the breast in all its arts, perhaps he would have coped much better with the isolation and adulation, but he was a truck driver: son of a sharecropper. He had to live and think on his feet. Is it surprising that sometimes he put a foot wrong?

He surrounded himself with a cocoon of courtiers, back-slappers and back-stabbers. Some were there for the grace and favours, but the closest were there because they loved him. They regarded themselves as friends. However, friendship implies equality, and at the court of the King, there is only one King. Ultimately, Elvis had only himself.

Elvis knew he had talent, wealth and power. But he did not know why it had been vested in him. A princeling born to be King

would have known better than to ask. Is it surprising that, like many a king, he often appeared to lose touch with reality?

It was not Elvis Presley who closed out reality, but reality that slammed its door in his face. From the age of nineteen he was the man to whom no-one said "No."

From the moment *Heartbreak Hotel* stormed to No.1 in the American charts, the story of Elvis Presley took on the aura of fantasy. It became the modern-day fairy tale. No Hollywood mogul would have scripted a story of such a rise from rags to riches before 1956 – it had never happened.

Elvis Presley managed during his life to be both one of the most reviled and most revered men of his time. In the 1950s he terrified parents as much as he tantalized their children. In the 1970s as a live performer he was revered by all, with a universal appeal. The most popular entertainer the world has ever known.

Apart from a few brief years in the 1960s, when the Beatles challenged the phenomenal popularity that had surrounded Elvis Presley for an entire generation, no other entertainer has ever rivalled – or is ever likely to rival – the mystical hold he had over people. Every year thousands of people still visit his home, Graceland, now revered by Presley fans as a shrine. Throughout the world there are innumerable fan clubs holding regular meetings and conventions, raising money for charity in the spirit of giving that dominated Elvis's life.

Elvis's record sales have topped one billion and more Golds are being created even now. He was the first entertainer to be shown worldwide by satellite – a show watched by more people than watched Man's first walk on the Moon. He also made 33 films – all of which made fortunes. He generated business totalling more than four billion dollars during his lifetime and more since his death.

At the time of writing, one of the pop megastars of the moment is Michael Jackson. If he continues to sell as he is doing he will eventually reach Elvis's total of record sales, **but it will take him 17 years**.

In life Elvis Presley became a legend. In death he has become a cult. The life, the legend, the cult was to end as it began. In tragedy. And in tears. It was a night in January in a little, wooden, two-room shack on the wrong side of the tracks in Tupelo, Mississippi, 1935.

OPPOSITE: *Concert and rehearsal shots from **That's The Way It Is.***

Chapter One

TUPELO

◆

"Since I was two years old all I knew was gospel
music and that music became such a part of my
life that it was as natural as dancing. It was a way to
escape from problems, my way of release."

Elvis

THE ELVIS DIARY
8 January 1935
Elvis Aaron Presley is born to farmworker Vernon Presley and his wife Gladys in a two-roomed wooden shack in Old Saltillo Road, East Tupelo, Mississippi. His twin brother, Jesse Garon, dies at birth.

25 May 1938
Hard times take their toll on the Presleys, and Elvis's father, Vernon, is sentenced to three years in Parchman Penitentiary for forgery.

January 1940
Elvis, now 5, begins his education at the East Tupelo Consolidated School. His singing voice is already making an impact on one of his teachers, Mrs Grimes.

Elvis Aaron Presley lay in his mother's arms in the bedroom. His brother, Jesse Garon, lay in a cardboard box in the kitchen. Jesse had been born 35 minutes before Elvis. Still-born. Mother and baby were sleeping, both exhausted by the ordeal of childbirth. The baby slept peacefully, the mother fitfully, her colour drained by grief, her cheeks streaked and stained by drying tears.

The door to the kitchen opened and a tall, big-boned but slim young man walked in, carrying a pail of water he had fetched from a hand-pump out the back. The only running water in the two-room wooden shack in East Tupelo trickled down the walls from the cracks in the leaking roof.

He poured some of the fresh water into a bowl for the doctor to wash his hands. He stared into the small fire, stared anywhere, stared everywhere. . . anywhere but at that makeshift cardboard coffin covered with a cheap patterned cloth.

The two men talked, the small-town doctor and the part-time sharecropper. They talked of the birth, the health of mother and child, the future and the fee. The share-cropper, Vernon, confessed he could not pay the $15 fee. He offered to work it off. The doctor nodded as he clicked shut his battered Gladstone bag. He might not get paid in cash, but he would get paid. . . in kind. These were honest, hard-working folk. Vernon would mend his fence, paint his house, chop some wood. It would never be better than cash, but it would always be better than nothing.

The doctor paused at the door, his hand on the latch. He looked at Vernon, who was sitting in a threadbare chair, slumped forward, arms on legs, gazing blankly at the flickering fire, and gestured towards the kitchen table.

"I'll make the arrangements," he said.

Vernon mumbled his gratitude.

The closing of the door sent a gust of wind gushing into the room, fluttering the tattered tablecloth, sparking the fire, rocking the naked light bulb which sent shadows swinging back and forth over the little coffin. Vernon buried his face in his hands. Tears seeped through his fingers as he recalled what the doctor had said. How could he break the news? How could he break her heart? How could he tell her? Not only had she lost a child. . . she could never have another.

The date was 8 January 1935 – a day that meant little to anyone but the young couple, Gladys and Vernon, who would commemorate it every year with fading memories of grief and growing feelings of gratitude and joy for Elvis. At first they were heartbroken. Both came from large, close families, and had expected the same for themselves. They didn't plan it, they just expected it. Children were not planned, they happened. Like leaks in the roof. And often just as welcome. Gladys and Vernon might have had four, five – even nine or ten children. And as Gladys came to terms with the news that she could never have another child, she determined that the love she would have shared unstintingly among ten, she would shower unreservedly upon her one.

Elvis became her world, her life. And she was his. She was to exert an influence over him that was never again to be repeated. For Gladys did not just give birth to Elvis Aaron Presley; she, more than anyone else, created ELVIS PRESLEY.

The Presleys and the Smiths had always been among life's losers. It was said that a David Pressley from England or Scotland or Ireland had settled in the Carolinas in the 1740s before moving west. Generations of illiteracy had changed the way the name was spelt, but never the way it was pronounced. It was in fact to become the most mispronounced word in the world.

Nobody knew where the Smiths came from – with a name like Smith nobody has tried too hard to find out – but it seemed that, like the Presleys, the Smiths had been around for ever, scratching a living in the Deep South. If either family had ever had money, it had been spent. If there had ever been land, it had been lost. If there had ever been good times, they had been long forgotten. There had only ever been work, hard times and, occasionally, hope.

The two families lived nearby in East Tupelo – an area of the town reserved for poor whites. Gladys, the second youngest of a family of five girls and two boys, lived with her parents on Berry Street, and Vernon lived with his parents, his brother Vester and three sisters in a two-room house on Old Saltillo Road. Vernon married Gladys after a brief courtship. He was 17 and she was 21, although some misplaced sense of machismo made Vernon claim

OPPOSITE TOP: *The shack in East Tupelo where Elvis was born.*

OPPOSITE LEFT: *Young Elvis with friends.*

OPPOSITE RIGHT: *Elvis with Vernon and Gladys.*

he was 21 and Gladys 19. Like their friends they would have married fleeing the restraints of parents and the poverty of their youth – eased a little now the children were grown and working. They might have dreamed a lot, but they could have expected little. . . just the nightmare of reliving their parents' lives: the search for a home, the unrelenting quest for a better life, for work, for food to feed an ever-growing, ever-hungry family. And then a few brief years of prosperity as the children grew, found work, provided money. . . and then left home to take their own place on the treadmill. This, too, was the promise life held for Elvis.

Even their smallest dream of leaving home was not to be fulfilled, and Vernon and Gladys moved in with Vernon's parents, and tried to save money on her wages as a shop girl and his as a trucker for a local dairy farmer who rejoiced in the name of Orville S. Bean. A little more than a year after they married, Gladys announced she was pregnant, and she was convinced it was twins. Now the search for a home became even more urgent – but just as hopeless.

Then Vernon injured his back in a road crash. Although this was to condemn the family to nearly 20 years of poverty, and Vernon to a lifetime of pain, at the time it seemed like a stroke of luck, for with the compensation Vernon received, he was able to build the two-room shack on Old Saltillo Road.

He built it high on stilts and blocks. It was either that or having to shovel silt from the shack when the nearby creeks overflowed their banks two or three times a year. It was a single storey house, 30 feet long, and sliced in two by a partition and chimney stack which served the bedroom as a fireplace and the kitchen as a cooker. The new timber soon warped, so that the doors had to be slammed shut and the windows often stuffed with rags to keep out winter winds, and the lavatory, like the only water supply, was outside and shared with neighbours. The only luxury was a narrow veranda, where Gladys, now too big to work, would sit shelling peas and swapping stories. It could have been worse. Not much, but at least they had their own roof over their heads and four walls and their families around them.

It was into this world of blind faith, ignorance and acquiescence that Elvis Aaron Presley was born that January morning in Depression-hit America. The new child put an almost intolerable strain on the finances of the Presley household. Gladys was not

THE ELVIS DIARY
3 October 1945
*Elvis, aged 10, enters and wins
second prize in a talent contest
at the annual Mississippi-
Alabama Fair and Dairy Show.
This is his first public
performance!*

8 January 1946
*Elvis is given a guitar by his
parents for his birthday, and
learns how to play it with the
help of Vernon and his uncle
Johnny Smith.*

working and they were relying on the meagre, spasmodic money earned by Vernon, who was unable to find regular work – much of the work available to a casual hand was heavy and Vernon, because of his recent back injury, could not manage it.

But the Smiths and Presleys were close (even more so now, since Gladys's sister Cletis had married Vernon's brother Vester), and when times were really tough they knew they had their families to fall back on. Every Sunday morning the delicate, dark-eyed young woman, her handsome blonde husband and their infant son would walk the short distance from their home to the First Assembly of God Church on Adams Street. It was little more than a wooden shack, little bigger than the Presleys' own wooden shack, but it was their only solace, their only refuge, their only entertainment. This was Old-time Religion, a potent mix of the Hell-fire fury of the Baptist and the good-time gospel of their black fellow-sufferers.

The congregation was encouraged, even expected, to collapse into religious euphoria on a high induced by the promise of Heaven and the performance of the preacher. The preacher would work himself and his congregation into a frenzy, jerking and swivelling his hips and rocking with his body. The generation of parents who raged at the gyrations of "Elvis the Pelvis" in later years, were being more than a little hypocritical. They had seen it all before. . . in church!

Nobody would have clucked or tutted or cast reprimanding glances as young Elvis, aged two or three, twisted free of his mother's arms, slid off her knee and ran down to join the choir. He may not have known the words. But, as he was to say later, "Even then I could carry a tune."

Elvis himself never underestimated the influence the Sundays, gospel and preachers had upon his music and his life:

**"Since I was two years old all I knew was gospel music and that music became such a part of my life that it was as natural as dancing. It was a way to escape from problems, my way of release.
In church I loved to hear the choir. My mother told me that when I was two years old I would**

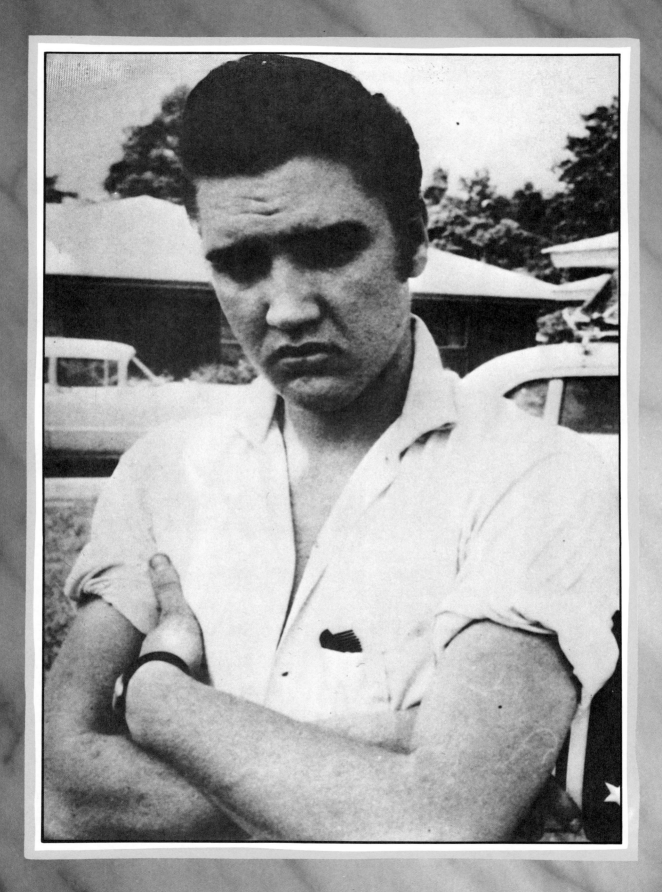

slide off her lap and stand there singing. . . I could carry a tune even though I didn't know the words. Maybe I wasn't always in tune but you could sure hear me above the rest. When I was four or five all I looked forward to was Sundays when we would all go to church, filled with sunlight and the security of my mother and father beside me. That was the only singing training I had. . . I never took lessons." *Elvis*

Sunday was the Lord's Day, a day of rest, but for Vernon too many of the other six days in every week were also days of rest. Finding work was getting no easier, and with the growing Elvis making ever greater demands, making ends meet was getting harder. As a result, Vernon, Gladys's brother Travis Smith, and a third man called Lether Gable conspired to forge a cheque – the victim being Vernon's one-time employer Orville S. Bean. The three men received about $200, made provision for their families and then left town for Texas in search of work. As a swindle it was amateurish; they had no hope of getting away with it. They were fools rather than knaves.

When money and work ran out in Texas they came home to face the music and the wrath of Orville S. Bean. They pleaded with him, begged to be allowed to pay back the money, to work off the debt. But with men scrapping to do a day's work for a handful of corn, cheap labour was the least of Mr Bean's worries. What he wanted was vengeance, though he called it justice. Consequently, the three men were sentenced to three years each on the notorious Parchman penal farm, where they were put to work picking cotton in the scorching sun.

But if things were tough for Vernon they were a whole lot tougher for Gladys and Elvis. As one of Elvis's cousins put it, "At least Vernon got to eat." Gladys and Elvis existed on hand-outs and hand-me-downs. She took in washing and sewing, she scrubbed floors, she picked cotton. Her man would have a home and family to come back to. Vernon's imprisonment and the family's ordeal had, if anything, brought the three of them even closer together. It was also to have another, profound effect on the family, and

particularly on Elvis. His mother had always stressed the need to be hard-working, honest and polite, and now Elvis knew why. When he was older, living on the mean streets of North Memphis, where as many kids went to reform school as to high school, Elvis always remembered the lesson of his father: prison held no romance or glamour for him, only the memories of hardship and shame.

One of the neighbourhood boys who grew up around Lauderdale Courts and knew Elvis from a distance, served time for theft. He said, "It is easy in a place like North Memphis to turn bad. You get into gangs, looking for trouble and easy money. Of course we never knew what Elvis would turn into but we always knew he would never turn bad. He never wanted to run with the gangs."

When he was released from Parchman, Vernon could have taken the easy way out – the highway leading straight out of Tupelo – but he was never that sort of man, and even had he wanted to, Gladys would never have let him. Vernon might have paid his debt to society. . . but he still had his debt to pay to the town. He returned to Tupelo and struggled to rebuild his life and good name.

In the beginning: Candid shots of Elvis the Rockabilly Rebel.

Life for the Presleys never did get much better in Tupelo. Gladys, over-protective as ever, rarely let young Elvis out of her sight. She would walk him to school in his faded dungarees and cotton shirts – patched but always clean – and then she would walk him home again. (Sometimes, feeling smothered by all this mother-love, Elvis would sneak off to the creek with a friend. He knew this was guaranteed a whipping and a lecture but he still did it.) Gladys was terrified something might happen to her only son – she doted on him. He also doted on her and always tried not to cause her too much concern.

Elvis was a spoiled child – at least, as spoiled as a child *could* be on a sharecropper's wages. The Presleys had little, but what little they had they gave to him – and a little more besides.

Elvis was never very special at school – neither in the classroom nor on the sportsfield – and he might never have been very special at anything if the family hadn't been poor. Elvis wanted a bike for his birthday, but, despite the sacrifices and the scrimping, when the day arrived Gladys had managed to put away only enough for a guitar. Elvis always remembered being disappointed that day – but grateful all the same.

Elvis loved cars, at the wheel of an early model he owned.

"I really wanted that bicycle but Daddy couldn't afford one, so he bought me a guitar that cost about 12 bucks. I know even that was a great sacrifice and he went without smokes for several weeks." *Elvis*

But Elvis was a Presley – and the Presleys were used to making the best of second best. He picked up a few chords from his uncles Johnny Smith and Vester Presley and a few more pointers from the radio. The family used to tune in to the gospel and country and western shows, but when he was on his own Elvis would twiddle the dial until he picked up the black rhythm and blues stations and listen in to the forbidden Race Music channels.

At school one day a teacher asked if any of the children knew any hymns. The normally shy Elvis, always reluctant to draw any attention to himself, volunteered to sing Red Foley's beautiful ballad *Old Shep,* about a boy and his dog. It was not a hymn as such, but sung by Elvis it was not far short. The teacher, Mrs J.C. Grimes, was so impressed with his voice and depth of feeling that she took Elvis, now aged about ten, to the Mississippi/Alabama Fair and Dairy Show in Tupelo and entered him in the local talent show. He was too short to reach the microphone and had to stand on a chair, but he won second prize and $5 worth of rides at the

Elvis and fans outside his home in Germany.

fair. This may or may not have been the beginning of Elvis's determination to become a singer, but it certainly was the beginning of his love of fairgrounds, which became a near obsession when he finally became a star.

But good times like these were few and far between – and becoming fewer still. The Presleys and the Smiths had always been migrant workers of a sort. One generation would move to a town, raise their families and then the children would move on, following a dream.

By now Vernon and Travis Smith had re-established their good names in Tupelo. That was all they owed the town. Like characters from *The Grapes of Wrath* they packed everything they had in their battered, broken-down cars. They left Tupelo with nothing – certainly not regrets, and very few pleasant memories.

"We were broke, man, broke. We left Tupelo overnight. Dad packed all our belongings in boxes and put them on the top and in the trunk of our 1939 Plymouth. . . Things just had to get better." *Elvis*

They did, but not before they got a whole lot worse.

THE ELVIS DIARY

June 1947
The still impoverished Presleys have by now moved into Tupelo itself. Vernon Presley gets a job driving a truck.

September 1948
Vernon loses his job and the Presleys move to Memphis. The family move into a one-roomed apartment in 572 Poplar Avenue, and Elvis is enrolled at the huge Humes High School.

Chapter Two

THE
MOVE
TO MEMPHIS

◆

"When a student did well he was invited to do an encore. Miss Scrivener said, 'They like you – go out there and do another song.' So I did. I sang *Till I Waltz With You Again*. At the end I heard this loud rumbling, which I supposed to be applause."

Elvis

Vernon pulled the old Plymouth off the highway on to the garage forecourt. It was a bright, sunny, autumn day, with no sign of cloud, but for the last two miles or so he had been driving with his wipers on. The radiator was red-hot and sizzling, spitting and steaming up the windscreen. This must have been the fifth or sixth time he had stopped to top it up. If he was cursing, it was under his breath. One or two more stops and they would hit Memphis. They would make it. And if they didn't make it, they would make out. They always had.

There was a bounce of optimism about Vernon as he replaced the cap, dropped the bonnet, grinned and waved at Travis who had tucked his car in behind the Plymouth. Vernon climbed behind the wheel and glanced across at Elvis and Gladys. Elvis was quietly singing some gospel tune and Gladys, her eyes closed, was nodding in time, a faint, indulgent smile creasing her cheeks. "We'll make it to Memphis," he vowed to himself. "And we'll make it in Memphis."

THE ELVIS DIARY
1 May 1949
Things look up for the Presleys. Vernon gets a job for the United Paint Company and they move to subsidized accommodation at 328 Lauderdale Courts.

November 1950
Elvis helps supplement his family's income by getting a job as a cinema usher at Loew's State Cinema.

Memphis greeted them with the sort of welcome a spider reserves for a fly. Elvis, wide-eyed and wide awake, marvelled at the colours, the crowds, the shops and sheer size of the place as they cruised the city streets looking for the kind of area that might offer rooms to itinerants.

They found it on Poplar Avenue. The area had once been the home of the barons in the Capital of King Cotton. The house was large, had been impressive and grand. Now it was run-down, near-derelict. The teeming dormitories of King Cotton's serfs.

There were 16 families, all sharing one kitchen, and one lavatory. The Presleys moved into one room and the Smiths took the one above. The house stank of damp, infested wood, infected beds and unwashed bodies. To open a window to allow the stench out was to let the stench in from the streets.

The next day the trudging search for work began. For the most part, the two families lived on turnip greens. Elvis and his young cousin Billy would raid the bins of the nearby grocer, carrying home the fruit and vegetables his customers would not buy, then Gladys would cut out the bad parts and make the most of what was left.

Travis soon found work and the Smiths moved out and up – into their own two-bedroomed apartment. The Presleys stayed,

Vernon still unable to find regular work, until the council found them a place in Lauderdale Courts. The Courts provided homes to needy families on welfare, or people earning a little above what they would receive on welfare. There was a sitting-room, two bedrooms, a kitchen and a bathroom. The Presleys had never known such luxury or the luxury of so much space.

Elvis enrolled at the nearby Humes High School. He found the grim three-storey building with its 1,600 strange, unfriendly faces intimidating. Always shy, a loner, he withdrew even more into the protective custody of his mother. He went unnoticed and that was the way he wanted it. It was not until he was 15 that anyone but Elvis and his parents would have even been aware that he went to Humes, so low was his profile.

And then, at 15, Elvis seemed to undergo a transformation. He became a teenager in the years before the word existed, at a time when there were only "young adults" or "juvenile delinquents". For years his mother had been telling him he was different, special, and it was as if Elvis had finally decided to prove he *was*.

To start with, he found himself a part-time job as an usher at Loew's State Cinema on South Main Street, working from 5 p.m. until 10 p.m. The 12 dollars 75 cents he earned was a welcome supplement to the family's income and went towards his clothes and pocket money, although Elvis would have worked there for nothing. He loved to lose himself in the darkness, identifying with the action and actors on the screen.

His idols were James Dean and Tony Curtis – two young heart throbs who played tearaways rebelling against the flannel-grey suits and empty grey lives of their parents – and, in the days when the no-nonsense crewcut was the rage, Elvis grew his hair long, Curtis-style, and carefully, lovingly and almost constantly combed the back into the don't-give-a-damn DA. He copied the turned-up collar, that was to become his trademark, from the swashbuckling films of the 1950s where the swordsmen always wore high-collared capes, and he started greasing his brown hair so that it looked two or three shades darker.

Elvis lost his job at the cinema after flirting with a girl and fighting with her boyfriend, and in the evenings he started wandering down Beale Street, a black area of Memphis acknowledged as the home of the Blues. He would stop at Lansky's clothing store – a shop that specialized in the gaudy,

vibrant colours so loved by the black community – and would press his nose against the glass, dreaming of the clothes he would buy if he ever had the money.

The owner of the store, Bernard Lansky, remembers seeing the odd-looking youth staring through the glass: "One time I went out and said, 'Come on in son. We don't charge for looking.' He mumbled 'No sir,' and pulled out his pockets to show they were empty. Then he said, 'But one day I'm gonna buy all my clothes at your store'. "

Elvis was as good as his word. When he started work he began buying all he could afford at Lansky's. When he started performing he was short of stage clothes, and short of the money to buy them, so he went to Mr Lansky and asked if he could have credit, paying back so much a week. Mr Lansky was pleased to oblige. In the years to come Elvis repaid that debt a thousand times, continuing to buy many of his stage outfits and casual clothes from an old friend.

But Lansky's was not the only attraction of Beale Street. The black quarter of the town was a different world to a young white boy – even one living in the slums of North Memphis. It was a world of magic. Black magic. A world of black, magical music denied to the whites by themselves out of bigotry and fear. It was the sound of empty bellies, raw, sensual, threatening, subversive. The sound of turnip greens, not home-baked apple pie.

Elvis would turn up his collar, thrust his hands deep into his pockets, swing his shoulders, curl his lip, hope he looked tough and stroll down Beale. He would step over the drunks, side-step the advances of the working girls and the pimps who spent their money. What he wanted they didn't have. He would stop outside an open window and listen to a mournful lament, outside an open door and listen to the pounding of rhythm and blues. All his life he had been immersed in gospel and country music. Now subconsciously, unknowingly, he was soaking up, straining, filtering, the last, lost chord of a musical revolution.

There's no doubt that if Elvis had any musical ambition at this time, it would have been to join a gospel quartet. When he was 16 he used to sneak off to the Ellis Auditorium to listen to an all-night gospel Sing, learning from the way the groups would work an audience. He said, "I remember I always had to go by myself because the other kids didn't like that kind of music." But apart

OPPOSITE ABOVE: *Elvis always rehearsed hard.*

OPPOSITE BELOW: *Standing outside his home in Audubon Drive, Memphis.*

from some vague ambition to join a gospel group, it is unlikely that Elvis seriously entertained any ambition towards earning a living from music. As Vernon used to tell him, "I know a whole lot of guitar men, but I don't know one who is worth a damn."

At Humes, Elvis was beginning to be noticed. His long, greased-back hair, the sideburns, the turned-up collar, the loud clothes. . . it was getting more and more difficult *not* to notice him. Among the girls there was a mixed reaction. Some thought, "He's weird – stay clear." Others thought, "He's weird - I'd like to get to know him." Among the boys the reaction was almost universal. . . "He's weird."

Elvis's refusal to accept crew-cut conformity led to attempts by some to bully him. But he was fit, wiry and street-wise, with a wild temper, and in a one-to-one confrontation he was more than capable of taking care of himself. But bullies roam in packs. Once, a group cornered him in the changing-room. Elvis knew he was in for a hiding. As the baiting reached a peak, the door opened and big Red West, star of the school football team, walked in. One look told Red what was going on, one look from Red sent the bullies scurrying. Red had no truck at the time with Elvis, but he had even less with bullies. After that Elvis and Red became firm friends. It was at this time that Elvis met another boy, who was to become a life-long friend. . . George Klein. George had an easy kind of charm, an easy way with words, and an easy way with girls. He was class president and the most popular kid in school. With George and Red by his side Elvis never wanted for friends.

George took to Elvis because of his wild vulnerability. . . and their mutual love of music. Most of their classmates wanted to be footballers, baseball players or athletes, but George wanted to be a disc jockey. And Elvis loved to sing. Sometimes George would persuade him to sing at parties, and Elvis would oblige reluctantly, head bent, eyes closed, as he strummed his battered guitar. It was in fact George who persuaded Elvis to sing in the school concert. He sang *Cold, Cold Icy Finger.*

"When a student did well he was invited to do an encore. Miss Scrivener said, 'They like you – go out there and do another song.' So I did. I sang *Till I Waltz With You Again*. At the end I heard this

THE ELVIS DIARY

December 1952
Elvis makes his second public appearance when a teacher at Humes, Miss Elsie Scrivener, encourages him to perform at the annual school Christmas concert.

April 1953
Elvis cuts his first "record" My Happiness at Memphis Recording Services (later to become Sun Studios). It costs him $4, and is a present for his mother, Gladys. The receptionist, Marion Keisker, is impressed enough to make a note of his name.

loud rumbling, which I supposed to be applause. After it was over, I said, 'They really did like me, didn't they, Miss Scrivener?' I was amazed at how popular I became at school after that concert."

Elvis

In the classroom at Humes – now set aside as a memorial to Elvis – there is a copy of the programme for that concert. About two-thirds of the way down is listed "Elvis Prestly". . . perhaps the last time his name was ever misspelled.

Elvis graduated from Humes in the summer of 1953. His had been an undistinguished school career – his only mention in the Year Book was his name beneath his picture, recording only for posterity that he had been there. Certainly not the school's choice for the Boy Most Likely to Succeed.

Shortly before Elvis left Humes, the family's fortunes seemed to take a turn for the better. Vernon had at last found himself full-time work as a packer at the United Paint Factory on Concord Avenue. Elvis found work too. When he left school he joined the Precision Tool Company. The family income now exceeded the breadline level permitted to residents of Lauderdale Courts. But they would have moved out with optimism. With two wage packets coming in, Gladys could look forward to a future that promised better times – and maybe even a new dress.

But Elvis's outrageous style of dress was to cause him trouble at Precision. Many of the other workers baited him about his long hair and trucker-style sideburns. The baiting got out of hand and he was given the ultimatum: Get it cut – or quit. Elvis quit.

They were now worse off than they had been since they first moved to Memphis because the rent they were paying at their latest apartment on Alabama was much higher. Gladys must have wondered if she would ever get a new dress.

But Elvis had never been a lazy boy. He had worked at a succession of part-time jobs as a schoolboy – his parents even bought him an old mower so he could earn pocket-money cutting lawns – and now he started haunting the employment office as he haunted Beale. He was out of work for about three weeks before a suitable job came up – as a driver for Crown Electric. The lady in the employment office looked Elvis up and down. He was bright,

ABOVE: *George Klein with Elvis.*

OPPOSITE: *The welcome-home concert in Tupelo.*

he could drive, he was a willing worker and so well-mannered. The job held the promise of a trade, and Elvis was ambitious. The job looked right for Elvis. . . but did Elvis look right for the job?

As Elvis mumbled "Thank-you Ma'am" and left the employment office for his interview, the lady made a discreet telephone call. The owner of Crown Electric, Mrs Gladys Tisler, remembers it well. "They told me they were sending out a young man for the driving job. They hedged around it a little and told me not to judge him too much on his appearance.

They said he had long slicked-back hair and sideburns but not to pay too much attention to that. He was really a hard-working boy with beautiful manners.

And that's the way he turned out. But I must admit if they hadn't taken the trouble to call and warn me, I would never have given him the job."

Elvis settled into the job delivering equipment to construction sites in a Ford truck. It paid him $1.25 an hour and he dreamed of the days he would earn big money as an electrician. But there were other dreams too. Elvis recalled, "When I was driving my truck and one of those shiny new cars went by, it started me dreaming. I always felt that someday something would change for me. I didn't know exactly what, but there was this feeling that the future looked kind of bright." It was during one of his delivery runs that Elvis first noticed a tiny, red-brick, single-storey building next to a parking lot on Union Avenue. A board in the window invited the people of Memphis to record their favourite poem, a song, a speech, baby's first word. All for $4.

The neon sign read: Memphis Recording Service. It was to become better known as Sun Studios. . . a cradle for such greats as Carl Perkins, Jerry Lee Lewis and Johnny Cash, but the hand that was first to make that cradle rock belonged to a young trucker with an unlikely name. . .

ELVIS PRESLEY.

THE ELVIS DIARY

June 1953
Elvis graduates from Humes. The Presleys leave Lauderdale Courts and take an apartment at 398 Cypress St.

July 1953
Elvis, now 18, takes his first full-time job at the Precision Tool Company, then leaves to work as a truckdriver for the Crown Electric Company.

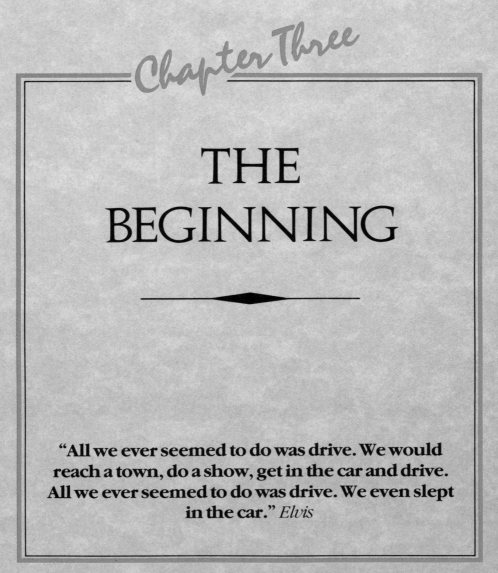

Chapter Three

THE BEGINNING

"All we ever seemed to do was drive. We would reach a town, do a show, get in the car and drive. All we ever seemed to do was drive. We even slept in the car." *Elvis*

THE ELVIS DIARY
January 1954
Elvis returns to the Memphis Recording Service to make another $4 disc. This time, owner Sam Phillips listens with interest and notes Elvis's address. The family have now moved again, to 462 Alabama St.

May 1954
Sam Phillips contacts Elvis and introduces him to two musicians who are to play an important part in his life — Winfield Scott ("Scotty") Moore and William Black. They will form part of Elvis's permanent backing group, The Blue Moon Boys.

Marion Keisker looked up from her desk in the small office at the front of the Memphis Recording Service. . . as she had done several times before in the previous ten minutes. He was still there. A long-haired kid with long sideburns in khaki overalls as greasy as his slicked-back hair.

Suddenly he darted for the door, pushed through as if he would push it down, and came inside as if he were being chased. The door slammed shut behind him as if he were hoping it would lock him in until he had finished what he had come to do.

Miss Keisker smiled to herself and got on with her work. They were all like this, these kids. . . full of hope, full of dreams. Full of nerves. Full of themselves. Full of talent. Most of them anyway. She looked down the line of would-be stars, nervously drumming their fingers on scuffed cases of well-strummed guitars. In Memphis it seemed that everyone could sing. Even the bullfrogs croaked in key. She wondered what this latest kid's excuse would be for cutting a record. . . a present for his girlfriend, his momma maybe. His momma probably. That was the usual one.

She was familiar with the excuses — and the real reasons. They wanted to know what they sounded like. Whether they really did have any chance of making it. And they knew that her boss Sam Phillips ran a small record label as part of his business, and that he was constantly searching for new talent. Not just any talent. A very special kind of talent. . . A white boy who could sing like a Negro. A white boy who could sing with the raw, sexy earthiness of the Negro. Not just sing a song, but feel it. "If I could find a boy like that, Marion," he had said a million times, "I could make a million."

The kid in the khaki and sideburns was at the head of the queue. "What's your name?" asked Marion.

"Elvis Presley, ma'am," the kid said in barely more than a mumble.

"What kind of singer are you?" she asked.

"I sing all kinds."

"Who do you sound like?"

"I don't sound like nobody."

"Hillbilly?"

"Yeah, I sing Hillbilly."

"Who do you sound like in Hillbilly?"

"I don't sound like nobody. I don't sing like all the rest," he said.

LEFT: *At a **Jailhouse Rock** recording session.*

RIGHT: *An early Memphis show.*

Elvis sang two numbers – *My Happiness,* a hit song of the time by the Inkspots, and *That's When The Heartaches Begin.* The session lasted little more than a few minutes. Elvis listened to the playback, and winced.

"What do you think?" asked Marion.

"Not much," replied Elvis. "I sound like someone banging on a bucket lid."

Marion Keisker did not agree. There was something about that voice, something she had not heard before. She kept a part of his take and filed it with a note: Elvis Presley. Good ballad singer. 462, Alabama Street. 375 630. Hold. (The Presleys could not afford a telephone. The number belonged to the family upstairs.)

There was another lady who did not agree that Elvis sounded like "someone banging on a bucket lid". . . his mother. Elvis recalled later, "She borrowed an old gramophone and played that record until it was plum wore out."

When Sam Phillips returned from lunch Marion Keisker played him the tape, but Sam heard the sound of nothing special. Certainly not the sound of a white who could sing black. Certainly not the sound of a million dollars.

Elvis heard nothing at all. In January of the following year, three days before his nineteenth birthday, he returned to the Memphis Recording Service. This time Sam Phillips was there. Elvis paid his $4 and recorded two more sides – *Casual Love,* a ballad, and *I'll Never Stand in Your Way,* a country song. Sam liked the sound of the sweet, strange, raw voice. There was something there, and yet there was nothing. Maybe if the right song came along. . . *maybe.* Sam made a mental note and, in the time-honoured show business fashion, told Elvis, "We'll call you."

With one difference. He *did* call, though not for some time later. And then only because he couldn't find the singer he really wanted. Someone had brought in a demo of a ballad called *Without Love.* It was sung by a young Negro boy – but nobody could remember his name. Sam wanted to use the song but he needed a singer. Marion Keisker suggested Elvis. Sam agreed and she called the number. According to legend, Elvis was down at the studio so fast, Miss Keisker had not even put the phone back on the hook before he was at the door.

Elvis listened to the song and then tried to sing it. It was awful. He tried again. Dreadful. Again. Painful. Again. Rubbish. Again. . .

LEFT: *A soothing mouthwash after a performance.*

RIGHT: *A rare shot of Elvis playing the drums.*

"Forget it," said Sam. "What can you sing – if anything?"

"I can sing anything," replied Elvis. He launched into his repertoire – country, gospel, Billy Eckstine, Eddy Arnold, Dean Martin. Sam must have wondered when he would get round to Doris Day. Elvis recalled: "I guess I must have sat there at least three hours. I sang everything I knew. . . pop stuff, spirituals, just a few words of everything I remembered." Sam never really knew why he decided to persevere with this weird kid with the weird-sounding voice. Maybe there was something there – if only he could dig it out. He brought in a country guitar player called Scotty Moore and Bill Black, a bass player, to round out the sound and to try a few songs, and night after night, week after week, the trio bounced songs off the walls of the tiny studio. They bounced right back.

Then one night – it was 5 July 1954, the hottest night of that year – Elvis started fooling around during one of the breaks. Perhaps he sensed that Sam was about to give up on him. Perhaps he just decided to sing the way he wanted to sing, rather than the way he thought Sam wanted him to sing. Perhaps the heat got to him. Whatever the reasons, he picked up his guitar and started beating up Arthur Crudup's *That's All Right Mama.* Bill Black on bass quickly joined in and then Scotty, not to be left out, picked it up. Elvis was jumping all over the studio. Sam raced out.

"What are you doing?" he yelled.

They shrugged their shoulders, a little shame-faced.

"Well whatever it is, don't stop," said Sam. "It sounds pretty damn good." The song sounded like a mixture of country and rhythm and blues but with something extra. At last Sam knew he had something.

Now the search was on for a song to back it. They found it – eventually – in *Blue Moon of Kentucky,* a country number. At first Elvis tried it straight. Then Bill Black started to beat it up. Sam turned on the tape. "Fine, man," he said. "That's different. That's a pop song now."

By accident, perhaps by design, Sam had created a masterpiece of marketing. On one side was a country and western song with an R and B feel. On the other was R and B with a country feel. At first, however, it looked as though the whole thing might backfire. The R and B stations found it too country, and the country stations found it too R and B.

Sam turned to an old friend, his namesake but no relation, Dewey Phillips, a DJ who ran a show on local Memphis radio called Red Hot and Blue. It was a mixture of everything – R and B, country and pop. Dewey was not afraid to play anything, and he was giving more and more air time to the black music that he knew – or sensed – would appeal to the white kids. Dewey agreed to play the record if Elvis agreed to be interviewed on the show. The first play choked the switchboards with callers wanting to know where they could buy the record. Sam hadn't even had any printed. The record really took off when Elvis was interviewed on the show. He was reluctant. "I ain't never done any interviews, sir," he told Dewey. "I wouldn't know what to say."

Dewey replied, "Just don't say anything dirty."

Dewey told him he would just chat to him before interviewing live on air and Elvis nodded, but, unknown to Elvis, Dewey had already switched on the microphone. Dewey later recalled,

---

THE ELVIS DIARY

5 July 1954
The three musicians record That's All Right Mama *for Sam Phillips. A "B" side is later found –* Blue Moon of Kentucky.

7 July 1954
Sam Phillips persuades a DJ friend of his, Dewey Phillips, to play Elvis's tape on his popular late-night radio show. Both this and Elvis's subsequent interview on the show are an instant success.

July 1954
Sam Phillips suggests to Elvis that Scotty Moore act as his manager and booking agent.

30 July 1954
That's All Right Mama *reaches No. 3 in the Memphis country and western charts. Elvis makes his debut as a public performer at The Shell in Overton Park, together with Scotty and Bill. The performance is an outstanding success.*

"When I told Elvis later that the interview was over and he realized he had been speaking live on radio he went pale and his knees buckled."

However, the real significance of the Dewey Phillips interview is the fact that Elvis talked about his school life at Humes High – at that time an all-white school. Suddenly the audience realized that Elvis Presley was a white boy. And many of the kids who would never have bought – have dared to buy – a record by a black singer, on principle, or on the principle of their parents, were now ringing through asking where they could get hold of it. Elvis was on his way.

Elvis never forgot the part that Dewey played in launching his career, and he always made sure that Dewey was the first to play his latest record. When Dewey died that privilege passed to George Klein, Elvis's long-time high school friend.

Sam had always deliberately avoided naming either side of the record as the A side, and it was now that this proved to be a smart marketing move: country programmes tended to stay with *Blue Moon,* while the R and B programmes plugged *That's All Right Mama.* The record was a hit in Memphis, reaching No. 3 in the local charts, but it also gained Elvis some national recognition. *Billboard,* the country's leading music paper, called Elvis "a potent new chanter who can sock over a tune for either the country or the R and B markets".

Elvis now had a hit record – albeit a minor one – but no experience of performing before a live audience. And the fans who were clamouring to buy his records were clamouring to see him perform. Perform what? He had only two songs. It was time for him to really get his act together – in more ways than one. Elvis, Scotty and Bill started rehearsing, trying to put a show together. They played at high schools, for peanuts or for nothing at all – mainly for the privilege of selling the record after the show. Sales soared, reaching well over 20,000.

The next problem was to find a record as a follow-up. They brought out *Good Rockin' Tonight* coupled with *I Don't Care If The Sun Don't Shine.* It didn't sell as well as the first, but this time *Billboard* called Elvis "a solid new singer".

The trio continued the tour of the high schools and Elvis continued his tour of Memphis while still delivering goods for Crown Electric every day. His success had meant no financial difference to him, but it had begun to make a difference of sorts for he used to hang out at a local record store in Memphis, lurking in the back to see how many people came in to ask for his record. One lunch hour he was in there, in the back as usual, when a crowd of kids came in. They asked for his record and the store owner happened to mention that Elvis was out the back and would they like to meet him. When he went to fetch him, Elvis had gone.

All this time, Scotty Moore had been acting as manager for the trio, but as the bookings increased he couldn't handle the performing, rehearsing *and* management, so Sam suggested a friend, Bob Neal, a disc jockey in his thirties with a lot of the right contacts. Bob started booking Elvis and the Blue Moon Boys, as he called them, further and further afield – small towns in Tennessee, Alabama, Florida and Louisiana. Eventually, Elvis quit his job. They bought a big car and hit the road.

"All we ever seemed to do was drive. We would reach a town, do a show, get in the car and drive. All we ever seemed to do was drive. We even slept in the car." *Elvis*

A valued shot of Elvis playing the piano.

One of Elvis's early appearances was at the Overton Park Shell in Memphis. The other acts had to have a whip-round for him because he wasn't a member of the performers union and didn't have enough cash to join. Elvis was on second from last. On last was the top of the bill, country star Slim Whitman.

Elvis went on, shaking with fright, especially as he was in front of his home audience and many of his old high school friends. His left leg started shaking. The fans went wild, and Elvis thought they were poking fun at him. He came off to thunderous applause. Slim Whitman, waiting in the wings, was heard to say, "How do I follow that?"

Then, through Sam Phillips, Elvis got the chance to perform on the Grand Ole Opry in Nashville. This was a national institution,

the Mecca of country singers, and it was Elvis's chance to really hit the big time, but response was less than enthusiastic from the staid, conservative red-neck audience. Jim Denny, whose job was to book the acts, told Elvis after the show,

---

"Son, you better go back to driving trucks in Memphis."

Elvis left Nashville with tears in his eyes. He said later, with a pain that never really eased, "That hurt, man, that really hurt."

Instead, however, Bob Neal booked Elvis for one night on the Opry's "poor relation" the Louisiana Hayride, another radio show without the prestige or audience of the Opry. The audience tended to be younger and less staid, and Elvis took the show apart. Booker and announcer Frank Page immediately offered him a year's contract for a once-a-week slot. It proved a wise move – every time Elvis appeared the show was a sell-out.

Elvis's third single was *You're a Heartbreaker,* backed with *Milkcow Blues Boogie* – but, again, it did not sell well, although he was continuing to pack in the crowds at live shows. Now at last he was making real money – but he never had time to spend any. Except on cars, and his family. It seemed that every six months Gladys and Vernon would move to a bigger and better house somewhere in Memphis. And the help was not just limited to his parents – any other member of the family who had hit hard times always knew they could count on Elvis's help.

The fourth single, with *Baby Let's Play House* and *I'm Left, You're Right, She's Gone,* confirmed Elvis as a star of the future. It was no longer a question of *if* but *when.* Bob Neal and Sam Phillips were both rapidly coming to the same conclusion: Elvis was becoming too big and too hot for them to handle. One night, after another smash on the Louisiana Hayride, Bob took Elvis aside and said, "Elvis, there is someone here I'd like you to meet –

" Elvis, this gentleman is Colonel Tom Parker. I think you're gonna get along just fine."

THE ELVIS DIARY

10 January 1955
Elvis takes on a new manager, Bob Neal, to replace Scotty Moore who can no longer cope with the commitments of performing and managing.

1 May 1955
Elvis and the Blue Moon Boys embark on their first major tour as part of Hank Snow's All-Star Jamboree. When Elvis appears at Jackson, Florida, there is a riot.

August 1955
Elvis makes his last record for Sun – Mystery Train, *backed with* I Forgot To Remember To Forget.

Chapter Four

ELVIS
MEETS
THE COLONEL

"My boy wouldn't do anything bad. He's a good boy, a boy who has never forgotten his church upbringing and he hasn't changed a bit."
Gladys Presley

THE ELVIS DIARY

October 1955
Start of a new tour, Elvis moves his parents into a new bungalow home at 1414 Getwell Road in Memphis.

2 November 1955
Mystery Train is No. 1 in the Country Charts—Elvis's first No. 1 record.

21 November 1955
Sam Phillips signs a deal for Elvis with R.C.A. Victor. The deal cost $35,000 plus $5,000 for Elvis.

Colonel Thomas Andrew Parker was a big man – a giant even among the men who ran the careers of the country greats who dominated the charts in the south-west states of America. He carried too much weight and his chins trembled when he laughed, which he did often and loudly. As well as an excess of flesh, he also carried a walking cane topped off with an elephant's head. Some people speculated it was the symbol of the Republican Party, though Colonel Parker was too canny to wear his politics on his sleeve – or in the palm of his hand. Others said it was a momento of his old days as a hustler, roustabout and barker with the carnivals and circuses. But a few said he chose the elephant's head just to remind people that he was one of life's heavyweights.

Certainly, everything about the Colonel was larger than life. Even his military title was honorary, bestowed on him by the Governor of Tennessee in 1953. But whatever the Colonel was – and nobody has ever really been sure – he was shrewd, smart, clever, crafty and knew the business. He was just right for Elvis – at just the right time. Elvis's manager Bob Neal had been having problems keeping up with Elvis at the time and had often turned to Colonel Parker to help with bookings further afield. Bob said, "He had gotten so big that it meant I would have to give up everything to go with him."

Bob had a wife, five boys, a job as a DJ – and a way of life he loved. He knew that staying with Elvis would mean giving up at least some of that – if not the lot. "I weighed it. I needed more time with my family. Elvis needed someone who could devote every moment of his time. I decided that it was not me," said Bob.

It was then that Bob introduced Elvis to Colonel Tom Parker. The Colonel had been successfully managing the careers of Hank Snow and Eddy Arnold, two country legends, but he had also been watching the career of Elvis with interest. He felt that Elvis had the potential to be something else – something nobody had ever seen before. He took every opportunity to watch Elvis perform, watched how his records did in the local charts, and commissioned reports from Presley concerts that he could not attend. What finally convinced the Colonel, however, was the success of *Baby Let's Play House* – the first Elvis record to make the national charts.

Bob Neal's contract on Elvis was coming to an end and the DJ

was in no hurry to renew it. The Colonel talked to Bob and knew he would present no problem – the only obstacle seemed to be Sam Phillips who held Elvis on a recording contract. But Sam was in the same situation as Bob – Elvis was becoming just too big to handle. Not only that but Sam needed money to develop some new talent he had uncovered – promising unknowns like Carl Perkins, Jerry Lee Lewis and Johnny Cash. So Sam gave the Colonel the go-ahead to negotiate the best possible deal.

But there was another obstacle that Colonel Parker had not considered – Elvis himself. Elvis was an intensely loyal man. Much has been written about his sense of honour and it is something that cannot be underestimated. He was under contract to Bob Neal and Sam Phillips and as far as he was concerned, he owed them everything. If Bob and Sam had not been willing to part with Elvis, there is no way Elvis would have ever parted with them.

Even with the OK from Bob and Sam, Elvis still had his doubts. He had taken to the Colonel right from the start, but he wanted a second opinion. The opinion of the person who had always protected and guided him, held him while he cried, comforted him when he had been afraid and unsure. His mother.

Mrs Presley took some convincing. Elvis had already made her richer than her wildest dreams. The Colonel persuaded her by promising that he would do for Elvis in business what she had done for Elvis in life. . . protect and cherish him. To Elvis he said, "You stay talented and sexy and I'll make amazing deals that will make us both as rich as rajahs."

Within a few months Colonel Parker had kept his word, kept every promise he had ever made to Elvis and Gladys. Elvis never doubted the Colonel again and gave him full and free rein over the business side of his career. But he always insisted – and the Colonel always conceded – on having full and free rein over the musical and performing side of his career.

Having received the final approval, the Colonel went ahead and negotiated the best possible deal for Sam Phillips. Eventually RCA signed Elvis in a $40,000 deal. Sam received $35,000 and Elvis $5,000 in lieu of royalties. With hindsight it seems a steal, but at the time it was the biggest deal for a comparatively unknown artist. Sam was pleased with the deal. It gave him the money to develop his other talents and in any case he estimated the professional life of any new singer as only about six months, and he was convinced

ABOVE: *Recording a Milton Berle TV show.*

OPPOSITE: *Off the set of* **Jailhouse Rock,** *with the Colonel and co-stars.*

OPPOSITE: *A still from* **Jailhouse Rock.**

he could find singers who would become as big or bigger than Elvis. In fact, shortly after the deal was struck, Sam released *Blue Suede Shoes* by Carl Perkins, which immediately became a monster hit. RCA called him and asked, "Have you sold us the wrong man?"

But if RCA had any doubts they were about to be very quickly dispelled. Elvis was in their studios recording a lot of material, including one song called *Heartbreak Hotel.*

On 5 January 1956, just three days before his twenty-first birthday and precisely two years after he had returned to Sam Phillips' studio to record his second 4-dollar disc, Elvis walked into the antiquated studios of RCA Victor in Nashville. RCA had a lot more space, and a lot more people, but their recording techniques were not a whole lot better than Sam's. However, out of improvisation came invention and originality. To get the haunted, echoing sound of *Heartbreak Hotel,* Elvis actually recorded the song standing in the stairwell.

The song had been written by Mae Axton, a long time associate of Colonel Parker. Some time before her co-writer, Tommy Durden, had pointed out a newspaper story about a man who had killed himself, leaving behind a note which included the line "I walk a lonely street." It was that line that inspired the song.

While Elvis was in the studio recording, Colonel Parker was sealing a deal that would give Elvis a run of six weeks on national television on the Dorsey Brothers Show. The programme was shown opposite the Perry Como Show and was suffering in the ratings. The producer Jack Philbin saw Elvis as "the guitar-playing Marlon Brando" – the symbol in America of rebellious youth. Brando's films were sell-outs, and Philbin was obviously hoping that Elvis would do for the Dorsey Show what Brando was doing for the cinema.

On his first appearance, Elvis sang *Heartbreak Hotel* and *Blue Suede Shoes.* The response was phenomenal and started the reaction that was to assure Elvis of a place at the top of the charts – and in history. Half the viewers demanded more of this sensational new singer. The other half demanded to see nothing more of him at all. He was lewd and degenerate – a threat to the morals of the country, they said.

Suddenly Elvis was the most talked about and controversial person in the United States. His record swept to the top of the

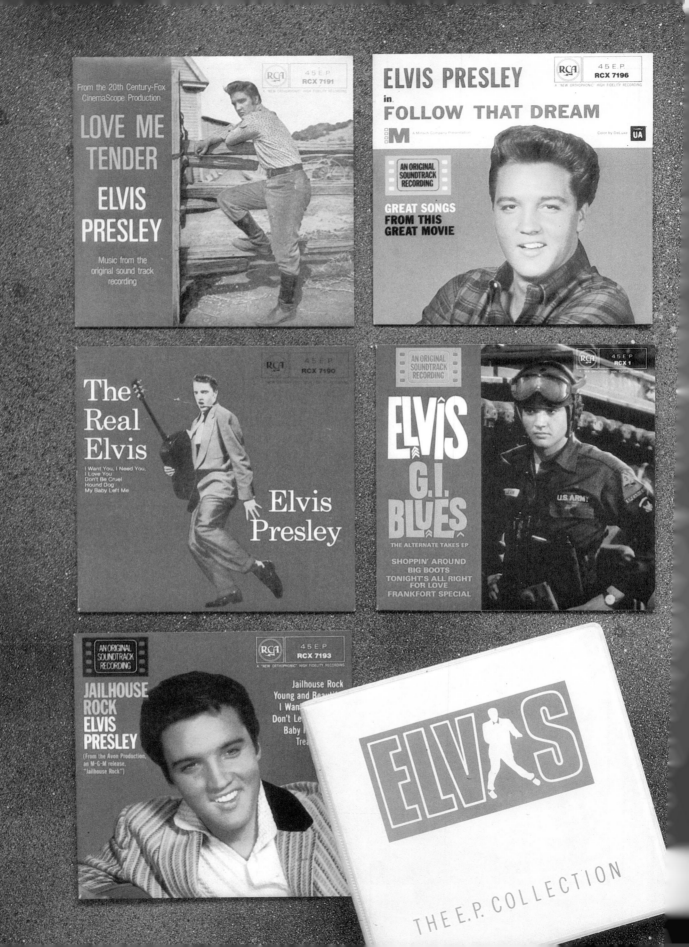

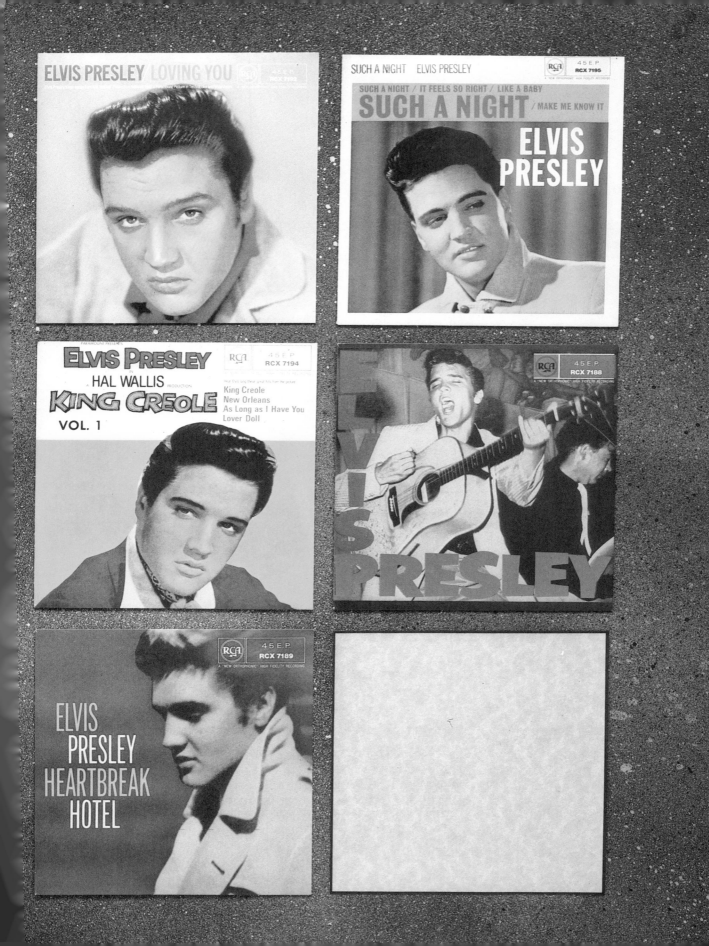

TOP: *Elvis receives a Triple Crown Award for* **Don't Be Cruel***.*

ABOVE: *With fellow recording star Johnny Cash.*

charts on 24 March, and everything Elvis sang, said or did was big news.

After his appearance on the Milton Berle Show, the rumbling of protest became a thunderclap of condemnation. But the more he was criticized by the establishment, the more he was lionized by the young. In San Diego more than 5,000 people paid more than $15,000 to hear him sing just eight songs. Not that they heard much – the concert was a riot. The police were called and a battalion of Coast Guards had to protect the singer from his fans. In Amarillo, Texas, young girls smashed in the plate glass window of a store and stole underwear for Elvis to autograph.

It seemed that *every* show was a riot – and often Elvis was lucky to escape with his life. His clothes were ripped from his back.

"Hell, I don't mind if the fans rip the shirt from my back, they put it there in the first place." *Elvis*

But it was after his appearance on the Steve Allen Show, however, that reviews reached fever pitch. One critic said "Mr Presley has no discernible singing talent. His speciality is rhythm songs which he renders in an undistinguished whine. His phrasing, if it can be called that, consists of stereotyped variations that go with a beginner's aria in a bathtub. For the ear he is an unutterable bore."

"He can't sing a lick, makes up for vocal shortcomings with the weirdest and plainly planned, suggestive animation short of an aborigine's mating dance." *A critic*

Evangelist Billy Graham said he would not let his daughter cross the road to meet Elvis Presley, and another reviewer said, "Watching him is like watching a stripteaser and a malted milk machine." One preacher called him the "whirling dervish of sex".

But Ed Sullivan, whose show was the biggest in the States, was forced to eat his words. He had previously said that he would never have Presley on his show. He now signed Elvis for a record-breaking $50,000 and the show received 82.6% of the ratings – 54 million people – a record that stood until the Beatles appeared on his show in 1964.

However, the reaction to his appearance on the Sullivan Show was just as vicious – even though Sullivan took the precaution of showing him only from the waist up. One critic wrote, "In some ways it is the most unpleasant thing I have ever seen."

Presley hysteria had inflamed America like a bush fire and it had all the makings of a bush war. In San Antonio, Texas, rock 'n' roll was banned from city swimming-pool juke-boxes to prevent kids dancing in their skimpy bathing suits. In New Jersey, all rock concerts were banned by a mayor after 25 teenagers were allegedly taken to hospital after a dance. In Massachusetts, after two teenage stabbings, a local lawyer said, "Tin Pan Alley has unleashed a new monster, a sort of nightmare of rhythm. Rock 'n' Roll gives young hoodlums an excuse to get together. It inflames teenagers and is obscenely suggestive." The *New York Daily News* suggested that teenagers should not be allowed to dance in public without the written consent of their parents, and called for a midnight curfew on anyone under the age of 21.

Elvis himself, in the days before his voice matured and gave him such an extraordinary range, was under no illusions as to where his real talent lay. "I'm not kidding myself," he said. "My voice alone is just an ordinary voice. What people come to see is how I use it."

"If I stand still while I'm singing I'm dead, man. I might as well go back to driving a truck."

In some ways Elvis did nothing to discourage his image as a sex-crazed monster. At one time he said, "They all think I'm a sex maniac. They're all frustrated old types, anyway. I'm just natural." He was also accused of signing autographs on the breasts of young girls. But he replied "I have written on arms, legs and ankles, any place decent where people can take soap and wash it off. I don't want no Daddy with a shot-gun after me." And when asked by a reporter about what he did when girls threw themselves at him, he replied, "I usually take them."

But more often his off-stage behaviour contrasted starkly with

---

THE ELVIS DIARY
15 March 1956
Colonel Tom Parker takes over the running of Elvis's career.

24 March 1956
Heartbreak Hotel *reaches No. 1 of the country and western and R and B charts. Elvis tours the country.*

his performance on stage. Presley the entertainer was wild and threatening to the mother of any young girl, but off-stage he was every mother's son. She would be proud to call him her own. He did not smoke, did not drink. His idea of a night out was a visit to the movies or the roller-skating rink. And he openly and obviously loved his parents, especially his Momma.

Privately, Elvis was stung by the critics – especially when the police filmed him to see if his performance constituted a public offence – and he asked his mother to speak out for him.

> **"My boy wouldn't do anything bad. He's a good boy, a boy who has never forgotten his church upbringing and he hasn't changed a bit".**
>
> *Gladys Presley*

The parents read her statement. Maybe this kid wasn't all bad after all. Why, hadn't he just bought his parents a brand new home out of his earnings?

The single-storey ranch-house on Audobon Drive, Memphis, cost Elvis $40,000, which he paid in cash. He then spent more on having a swimming-pool installed, together with a wall topped with spikes to keep out the fans, who were now besieging his home 24 hours a day whether he was there or not. One enterprising young lad a few doors away actually sold space on his father's prized lawn as parking places for the kids' cars.

A deputation of residents clubbed together and raised enough money to buy the house. Elvis did a little research and discovered he was the only one in the street who actually owned his home outright. He put in a counter-bid. . . offering to buy out the other residents of Audubon.

It was around this time that Elvis received another offer. . . and this one he found considerably more appealing. It came from a man called Hal Wallis. He was on the phone, calling from Hollywood. . .

Chapter Five

THE
EARLY
FILMS

◆

**"I was a powerful admirer of James Dean. I think
he was one of the greatest actors I have ever seen."**
Elvis

THE ELVIS DIARY
April 1956
Elvis flies to Hollywood to make a screen test at the invitation of Hal Wallis at Paramount. The result of the test is a seven-year contract for three films.

3 April 1956
When in Los Angeles, Elvis appears on the well known Milton Berle Show, and is watched by 40 million people.

23 April 1956
Elvis makes his debut in Las Vegas, but the audiences are different from what Elvis is used to, and the shows are not a success.

ABOVE AND OPPOSITE:
Scenes from Jailhouse Rock.

Hollywood never allowed Elvis Presley to fulfil his promise as an actor – he became a victim of his own phenomenal success. It was a well-known fact that Elvis Presley in a home movie – let alone a Hollywood movie – was a guaranteed money-spinner. Producers, like most other people, don't like to work any harder for their money than they have to, and with Elvis in a film it was easy money.

This attitude, aided eventually by Elvis's disinterest, was to lead to a succession of vehicle movies that had just one thing going for them – Elvis Presley – but it was an attitude that belied, and ultimately denied, the consummate acting skill that Elvis quickly and naturally developed during his first four, and probably best, movies.

The phone call from Hollywood invited Elvis to do a screen test. Hollywood wanted to see if Elvis could act. It would not have mattered whether he could or not. If the fans would pay to buy his records, pay to see him perform, pay to buy bubblegum, lipstick, perfume, powder, shoes and socks that carried his name, then sure as hell they would pay to see a giant-sized Elvis on the screen. Hollywood wanted a slice of this cake. The screen test was just motion pictures going through the motions.

In the test, Elvis played opposite veteran actor, Frank Faylen. The scene chosen was from *The Rainmaker* and Elvis was dressed in jeans, a work shirt, socks but no shoes. One old Hollywood hand described that test as "the best I have ever seen" and another said, "There's a natural quality about his acting. He acts the way he sings." Hal Wallis was equally impressed. He saw what he was looking for . . . the presence, the electricity that Elvis exuded on stage, was there on the screen.

Elvis was cast as Clint, the youngest of four brothers in a story set at the end of the American Civil War. As the youngest he is left behind to tend the family farm while the three older brothers go off to fight. The eldest brother, Vance, played by Richard Egan, is reported killed and Clint then marries Vance's sweetheart, played by Debra Paget. But Vance returns and at the end of the film Clint dies in a shoot-out protecting his older brother.

Originally called *The Reno Brothers,* the film was not scripted with any songs, but as soon as Elvis was cast they hurriedly wrote in four, three of which were *We're Gonna Move, Let Me* and *Poor Boy*. The fourth song, *Love Me Tender,* sung hauntingly by the

"ghost" of Elvis over the closing credits, became the film's title. It was a shrewd move by Hollywood as *Love Me Tender* was already top of the charts.

The film was remarkable in many ways – apart from being Elvis's first:

- In New York thousands of fans queued all night to get tickets for the première of *Love Me Tender,* including 400 girls who played truant from school. Every available police officer was put on duty in the area surrounding Times Square and the Paramount Theatre to control the crowds – and look for runaway minors.
- For most films about 200 copies are distributed at any one time, but with *Love Me Tender,* Hollywood made more than double that number available.
- The film was such a runaway success that the million dollars spent on its production was recouped within three days of its release.
- It was the only film in which Elvis "died". So many fans were outraged and genuinely distressed when they saw Elvis dying on the screen, that Hollywood decided that he would never again die in a part. (Even today, many Elvis fans refuse to watch the film or switch off before the death scene they find so harrowing.)
- *Love Me Tender* eventually grossed six times what it cost.

The fans loved the film. The critics hated it. But they were out of step. About a generation out of step. One critic wrote, "Is it a sausage? It is certainly smooth and damp-looking but whoever heard of a 172 lb sausage, 6 feet tall? Is it a Walt Disney goldfish? It has the same sort of big, soft, beautiful eyes and long curly lashes, but whoever heard of a goldfish with sideburns? Is it a corpse? The face just hangs there limp and white with its little drop-seat mouth."

He continued in the same vein, "A peculiar sound emerges. A rusty foghorn. A voice? Words occasionally can be made out GOAN . . . GIT . . . LUHHV . . . and then all at once everything stops and a big trembly tender half-smile, half-sneer slowly crosses the Cinema-Scope screen. The message that millions of US teenage girls love to receive has just been delivered." As a critique it seems more inspired by envy than objectivity. But it was like trying to put

---

THE ELVIS DIARY

5 June 1956
Elvis's second appearance on the Milton Berle Show, on which his hip-wiggling is considered outrageous.

2 July 1956
Elvis records three more songs at RCA. One of them, Hound Dog, will be his biggest hit single of the 1950s.

4 July 1956
The "Elvis Presley Show" takes to the road for a series of one-night stands. Elvis gives a big charity benefit show at the Russwood Stadium in Memphis and faces his biggest ever audience of 14,000 people.

9 September 1956
The extent of Elvis's fame is demonstrated when more than 54 million people tune in to watch him on the Ed Sullivan show.

26 September 1956
This is declared "Elvis Presley Day" when Elvis returns to Tupelo to perform at the Alabama-Mississippi Fair and Dairy Show.

OPPOSITE: *A publicity shot for* **King Creole,** *with Carolyn Jones.*

ABOVE: *Re-styling the famous D.A.*

OPPOSITE: *Elvis loosens up on a train between shows.*

THE ELVIS DIARY
24 October 1956
Variety *first gives Elvis the title of "King of Rock 'n Roll".*

16 November 1956
Love Me Tender *opens in New York to an ecstatic reception from fans.*

out a fire by blowing on it. The harder they blew, the hotter it grew.

Elvis launched into filming his second movie, *Loving You,* in which he played singer Deke Rivers, in a story based quite closely on Elvis's own rise to fame and most memorable for capturing something of Elvis's raw and original stage magic. Elvis loved his Hollywood career at this time. He once said, "I like singing but I love acting." Hollywood had introduced him to a new lifestyle. Performing had always forced him to be a night owl – now he was expected to be up at the crack of dawn. But there was one thing he did not like . . . Hollywood kept him away from his home and his momma. He often used to charter a plane to fly home for a few hours to see her.

The critics lashed *Loving You,* just as they had *Love Me Tender.* Elvis cried . . . all the way to the bank. He had picked up $150,000 – and that was before he started counting the royalties on the record. Then Elvis made what was to be his last television appearance before he was drafted into the American Army – his third and final appearance on the Ed Sullivan Show. Thousands of kids laid siege to the New York Theatre. Mounted police were called out in an attempt to control them and streets were cordoned off in an area covering seven blocks, while Elvis, wearing a gold lamé suit, sang a gospel song, *Peace in the Valley,* and *Don't Be Cruel.* Ed Sullivan came on and said, "I want to say to Elvis Presley and the country that this is a fine decent boy and we have never had a pleasanter experience on our show with a big name than we have had with him." It was the first, almost

OPPOSITE: *Elvis eating the famous welcome-home cake on being de-mobbed from the army (see page 95).*

imperceptible twist in Elvis's career, that was to turn him from just a teen idol into a national institution. Maybe the kid wasn't all bad after all . . .

Elvis started work on his third film, *Jailhouse Rock,* for which he was to be paid $250,000 plus 50 per cent of the profits. It was a meaty, dramatic part with a great score. Even the critics had to admit it wasn't bad. They were beginning to take Elvis a little more seriously. Comparisons were being made between Elvis and another teenage cult figure, James Dean, who had died in a car crash. It was even being suggested that Elvis might play the part of Dean in a movie about his life and tragic death. Elvis said at the time, "I was a powerful admirer of James Dean. I think he was one of the greatest actors I have ever seen. He and Marlon Brando and a whole bunch more I could call. But I'm not going to try and copy anybody. I'm trying to be myself in my acting, with my own name and my own style of acting."

Elvis's popularity was now so vast that his fame had become something of a myth – often with hilarious results. When he was filming *King Creole,* Elvis and his party took over the entire tenth floor and for security reasons the lifts were not allowed to stop there. One day, after shooting, Elvis returned to the hotel and walked into the lift with some friends. They asked for the tenth floor but the attendant said he was unable to stop there because Mr Elvis Presley, the entertainer and film star, was staying there. Elvis said, "Yeah, I know. I'm Elvis Presley." The attendant looked at Elvis, recognized him, and said, "I'm sorry, sir, I can't stop on the

ABOVE: *At the famous Music Gates at Graceland, talking to the fans.*

THE ELVIS DIARY

19 March 1957
In an attempt to find privacy, Elvis buys Graceland in Memphis. This will be his home for the rest of his life.

1 May 1957
Elvis starts work on Jailhouse Rock, *for MGM.*

20 December 1957
Elvis hears that he is to be drafted into the American Army.

*SINGING: **Baby, I Don't Care.***

tenth floor – even for you." Elvis had to take the lift to the eleventh floor and walk down!

Living in the house on Audubon Drive had proved impossible, a security nightmare. While Elvis could endure the attentions of the neighbours who hated him, he found it impossible to endure the attentions of the fans who loved him, so he started looking for a home which could afford him the privacy he craved and – for the sake of his health – desperately needed. He found it in a sandstone mansion, set in 14 acres of countryside around Memphis. Aptly named Graceland, it was to become Elvis's retreat, his refuge, his haven, his home... and eventually his prison. It was also to become the second best known house in America after the White House.

Elvis paid $100,000 for Graceland – half of which came from the sale of the house on Audubon Drive, but the cash payment was really just a down-payment of the money Elvis was to lavish on Graceland over the years. He installed security cameras and monitors and hired guards to help keep out the hordes of fans who besieged the estate day and night. He used to watch the monitors and, occasionally, when a particularly pretty girl caught his eye at the gates, he would ring through to his Uncle Vester Presley in the gatehouse and tell him to send her up.

The famous gates, featuring the rock 'n' roller and the notes of music, cost $2,400 and were a special rush order specially designed for Elvis by Abe Sauer. The house itself – built as part of a farm in 1939 and named after the owner's Great Aunt Grace – originally covered 10,000 sq ft, but with extensions Elvis built, it now covers 25,000 sq ft. He added the Trophy Room, the racquetball courts, the barn, an apartment for Vernon and his second wife Dee and several outbuildings. It had 21 rooms – nine of which were bedrooms – but the most stunning room is still the Trophy Room, where Elvis displayed all the awards he won in more than 20 years at the top in show business. On display are 55 platinum and 102 gold records, 63 gold singles, 26 platinum albums and 37 gold albums. There are also framed letters from Presidents Johnson and Nixon and another from FBI director J. Edgar Hoover.

Vernon had wanted to buy a home in Hollywood – which made sense, considering the amount of time Elvis was spending filming – but Gladys was reluctant to leave Memphis, her friends and relatives. It is likely that if Graceland had not come on the market,

Elvis would have been lost to the city he had come to regard as his home.

Gladys loved Graceland, although she often felt lost in its opulence. To make herself feel more at home she would send one of Elvis's cars out to North Memphis to collect a party of friends for a chat, and she still insisted on shelling peas sitting out on the porch.

Elvis himself was able to spend only a little time there since his Hollywood, television and performing commitments kept him away from home a lot. But when he *was* home, Elvis played – and played hard. He was unable to take his pleasures like ordinary people. His two favourite activities were roller skating and going to the cinema, and he used to have to hire a cinema or a skating rink in the early hours of the morning. With friends like Red West and Billy Smith he would take over a cinema until dawn. Fans who had heard that Elvis was hiring the cinema would hang around outside and Elvis would often invite them in – on the understanding they did not trouble him while he was watching a film.

Elvis's favourite games, however, were reserved for the roller skating rink. They used to play "Crack the Whip" – a game that would have given Hollywood and Colonel Parker apoplexy had they known about it. Elvis and his friends would join hands, form a line and skate round and round in smaller and smaller circles at frightening speed. Anyone on the end – and it was often Elvis – who let go would get hurt. Another game was called "Kill". Two sides would skate towards each other and deliberately collide with an opposing skater. The object was to see who had the most skaters standing at the end. Somebody was injured almost every time they played. The Guys made certain that nobody laid into Elvis too hard – although Elvis became angry if he thought he was getting an easy time.

It must have seemed that nothing could halt Elvis's ever-escalating good fortune. He was truly the singer with the Midas touch – everything he touched turned to gold records. He had conquered Hollywood. He had conquered the world. He was the most popular singer the world had ever known.

And then, one winter morning a buff-coloured envelope arrived with the thousands of fan mail letters. Its message was blunt, brisk and devastating. It said simply: Uncle Sam Needs You.

THE ELVIS DIARY

20 January 1958
Elvis reports at the Memphis Draft Board and is declared A1 medically. He is given a 60-day deferment to make King Creole.

23 January 1958
Elvis travels to Hollywood to begin shooting King Creole.

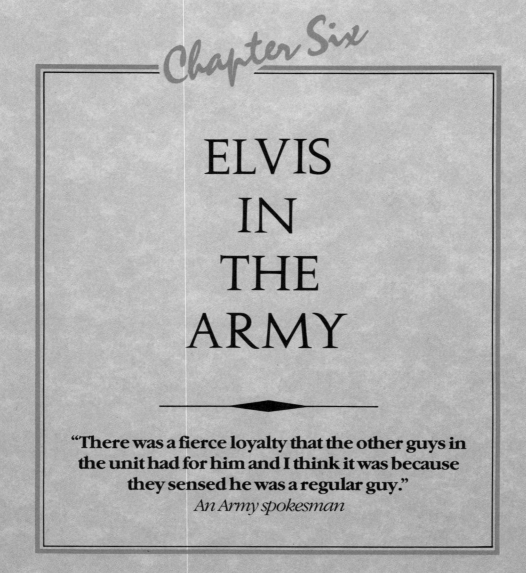

Chapter Six

ELVIS
IN
THE
ARMY

◆

**"There was a fierce loyalty that the other guys in
the unit had for him and I think it was because
they sensed he was a regular guy."**
An Army spokesman

ABOVE LEFT: *Being mobbed off-duty.*

ABOVE RIGHT: *A welcome break while serving in Germany.*

OPPOSITE: *On parade.*

Elvis Presley first felt the uncomfortable, chilling blast of the United States draft board while he was working on the film *Love Me Tender*. He was sent a circular asking him to "bring his status up to date." From that moment on, Uncle Sam was at war. . . with an army of hostile Presley fans who believed it was a government plot to "assassinate" the career of the leader of the youth revolution.

In January 1957 he was ordered to present himself for a medical check. He was pronounced A-profile. In Army jargon that meant Elvis was A1 and could expect his call-up papers. It was then that the fans went into battle on – but not *at* – Elvis's behest. Elvis made it clear right from the start that he was more than prepared to do his time in the Army – even at the expense of his career.

It seemed unthinkable that Elvis could be busted overnight from King to buck private. His fans organized a country-wide petition demanding that Elvis be designated a "national treasure" to prevent him being drafted. One fan wrote to the draft office in Memphis, "You wouldn't draft Beethoven, would you?" Elvis's critics, on the other hand, expected him to dodge the draft in

some way. Certainly, *everyone* believed that even if Elvis was not given special dispensation, he would take the easy way out and join Special Services – like many stars before him – which would allow him to live as a civilian while performing certain duties for the Army, like entertaining troops.

The United States Navy, hearing that Elvis was about to be drafted, approached him with a special offer if he would only sign on for them. They proposed to form a special Elvis Presley Company comprising other boys from Memphis. Elvis said "Thanks – but no thanks." He would take his chances with the draft.

Milton Bowers, chairman of the Memphis draft board, became the target of the Save Elvis campaign. He was receiving as much hate mail as Elvis was receiving fan mail. Eventually, at the end of his tether, he exploded: "I am fed up to the teeth. I eat, sleep and drink Elvis Presley. With all due respect to Elvis, who is a nice boy, we have drafted people who are far, far more important than he is."

Elvis himself seemed to be taking the whole thing a lot more philosophically than anyone else. He said, "I reckon I'll be able to

THE ELVIS DIARY

24 March 1958
Elvis begins his Army life in Fort Chaffe, Arkansas.

May 1958
He is given two weeks' leave from the Army during which he returns to Memphis for the première of King Creole. He installs his parents in 609 Oak Hill Drive, Killeen, Texas.

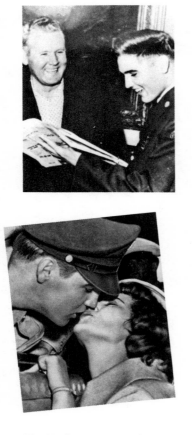

Top: *With Vernon Presley.*

Above: *Private Presley arrives in Germany!*

handle the Army assignment OK. I've been working since I was 14 – had to. I've worked in factories, drove a truck, cut grass for a living and did a hitch in a defence plant. I'll do whatever they tell me and I won't be asking for any special favours." He was just as philosophical about his career prospects when he had finished his tour of duty. "I hope my fans will welcome me back – maybe I'll start a new career as a ballad singer or a singer of spirituals."

There seemed to be only one serious obstacle to Elvis joining the US Army – money. Elvis would be taking a drop in salary from $100,000 a month – to $78. And it was calculated that the loss to the US Government in taxes would be about $400,000 a year.

Colonel Parker took a deep draw on his cigar, puffed out his chest and announced, with military authority, that, "I consider it my patriotic duty to keep Elvis in the 90 per cent tax bracket while he is in the Army." It was not to prove too difficult for the Colonel to keep his word. He had already arranged a deal with RCA to pay Elvis $1,000 a month during service. They had 50 per cent of the profit of *King Creole* which had not at that time been released; they also had the royalties on the songs from the film and there was to be one more recording session before Elvis went overseas.

Colonel Parker's cigar glowed brightly in the dark as Elvis arrived at 6.30 on a cold and wet March morning at the Memphis draft board to join the Army. The Colonel, never one to miss an opportunity, was handing out balloons to fans and pressmen advertising the about-to-be-released *King Creole*. The Army, never ones to miss an opportunity to boost recruitment, had agreed to co-operate with the Press to record Elvis's enlistment and the first few days of his new career. Elvis was given a medical at the Kennedy Veterans Hospital and then sworn in. He was given the number U.S. 53310761. Elvis Presley was now Private Presley. He climbed aboard a bus with the other recruits to drive to Fort Chaffee, Arkansas. The following morning the newsmen were up at the crack of dawn to picture Elvis tucking into an Army breakfast of sausage, egg, toast and coffee. Then it was on to a series of aptitude tests to determine in which branch of the Army Elvis would be most useful.

The event everyone had been waiting for took place after lunch. It was to be the most famous haircut since Delilah took a pair of shears to Samson and it was a moment that must have given his critics a lot of satisfaction. Elvis – or his hair, anyway – was being cut down to size. As the sideburns hit the floor, Elvis quipped, "Hair today – gone tomorrow." The world's press clamoured for before and after shots and in the confusion Elvis forgot to pay the 65 cents for the haircut. When he was called back he gave barber, James Peterson, a dollar – but forgot his change.

Later that day, it was announced at a press conference that Elvis would do his basic training at Fort Hood, Texas, with the 2nd Armored Division.

The pending call-up posed the biggest-ever threat to Elvis's career. A two-year enforced absence could kill him off as a pop idol, especially in a business where to last even a year was to last for ever. Elvis and Colonel Parker had to take a decision that, either way, could be make or break. The two-year absence could kill him. But not as certainly as any sign that Elvis thought himself too big, too good to serve his country. All over the United States young men of Elvis's age were being drafted. How would their sweethearts feel as they watched their boys march off in uniform, if Elvis stayed behind. How long would he remain their idol? And the parents?. . . would it not just confirm everything they had ever thought about this wild, sneering, sex-mad monster of mayhem, who was seducing their daughters and destroying the moral fibre of the country?

Inveterate gambler Colonel Parker took the biggest risk of his life. Elvis would not fight the draft. He would join the Army, and he would join as a buck private. No Special Services. No special treatment. His decision turned out to be a masterly stroke, silencing Elvis's more venomous critics and making fans out of people who had been buying his records for the sole satisfaction of smashing them to bits. It also laid the foundation for a wider, more broadly based career for when Elvis returned from service. It was to destroy Elvis, the Hillbilly Cat, but it was to make Elvis an all-round performer, with an all-round appeal. And it had the added advantage of giving him a rarity value. Colonel Parker had no choice but to believe that after his two-year exile, the King would rally his subjects and rout the pretenders in a glorious restoration.

Elvis was asked how the other recruits were treating him and he replied, "They've been swell – they treat me like everyone else and they consider themselves for what they are. Just GIs the same as me. That's how I see it."

THE ELVIS DIARY

8 August 1958
After a marked decline in Gladys' health, Elvis sends her back to Memphis where she is diagnosed with hepatitis and is moved to the Methodist Hospital. Four days later Elvis is summoned to the hospital.

14 August 1958
Gladys dies of a heart attack, aged 46. Elvis is grief-stricken.

22 September 1958
Elvis is posted to Germany.

1 October 1958
Elvis arrives in Bremerhaven Germany.

The Army called "Halt" on the publicity sessions a week later when Elvis arrived at Fort Hood for two months of intensive and tough training. But of course a military order could not stop the civilian fans. The base's switchboard was thrown into chaos by fans ringing non-stop on the off-chance they might be put through to Elvis and at weekends they laid siege to the base in the hope they might just catch a glimpse of Private Presley.

After two months' training Elvis returned to Memphis for two weeks' leave. It gave him the chance to attend the local première of *King Creole* and to slip up to Nashville for a recording session – the only one of his Army career.

The whole film had been put into jeopardy by Elvis's call-up. Paramount Pictures had invested $300,000 in the film before Elvis had stepped on the set. A January call-up would have meant the whole project being shelved. Elvis asked for and was granted a deferment until March – the only favour he asked or received from Uncle Sam.

King Creole was perhaps the pinnacle of Elvis's early career. The critics loved it and at last acknowledged that Elvis could act. The film, generally accepted as Elvis's best, was based on the Harold Robbins best-seller *A Stone for Danny Fisher* and was directed by Michael Curtiz who had directed the classic *Casablanca*. In it Elvis played Danny Fisher, a waiter and singer, who becomes involved with a group of gangsters. With support from Walter Matthau and Dean Jagger, the film was not only packed with great songs, but was also considered a dramatic success. *King Creole* established Elvis not only as a pop idol but as an actor of enormous potential. It was also to leave the fans breathless and gasping for more. More than anything else, *King Creole* created a demand for Elvis after the Army.

In Nashville, Elvis took the precaution of recording a little insurance – when added to the soundtrack of *King Creole* it gave RCA a nice little bankroll – but basically the Colonel was sticking to his strategy of a low profile for Elvis which would keep the fans ravenous for more. Elvis returned to Fort Hood and was allowed to live off-base with his parents in a three-bedroomed house. Gladys's health was beginning to worry Elvis and Vernon and when her condition deteriorated Mr and Mrs Presley returned to Memphis to be near her own doctor.

Gladys had never truly come to terms with Elvis's success and the changes it had wrought on their lives. She wanted to look her best for Elvis but she could not shake off her excess weight. She turned to diet pills and drink for solace. Elvis's absences from home, touring and filming, upset her and, despite his success, fortune and fame, she must often have wished he had become an electrician, settled down and started raising a family. Her son's enlistment into the Army and the prospect of his "going to war" would have been too much for her to bear. It must have been a factor in her deteriorating health.

Only a few days after arriving in Memphis, Vernon phoned through to Elvis. Gladys had been admitted to the Memphis Methodist Hospital and the doctors had diagnosed hepatitis. Elvis was granted emergency leave and caught the next available plane to Memphis. It was 11 August. Elvis stayed by her bedside non-stop for 36 hours, willing her to get well. On the evening of the 13th, totally exhausted and desperately needing a break, Elvis left the hospital. He went to a movie with his cousin Billy Smith and then back to Graceland to sleep.

Elvis tossed and turned in his bed, sleeplessly, restlessly. His cousin Billy Smith brought a few pillows, cushions and blankets and tried to sleep on the floor. As in the previous two days, there was to be no sleep for Elvis on 14 August 1958. In the early hours of the morning Billy took a call from the hospital. It was Vernon. Elvis had better get to the hospital right away. Vernon said nothing more, but Billy knew in his heart that Gladys was already dead. They drove to the hospital, jumping lights. Elvis ran into the hospital, straight into Vernon's arms. Vernon whispered. "She's gone son. She's gone." Elvis went into Gladys's room and threw himself across her body. He was inconsolable and wept convulsively. For days he was in a haze of bitterness and confusion. The Army granted him an extension of leave as news of his grief spread throughout the world. At the funeral he wept openly. Gladys was just 46.

"All I ever had is gone."
Elvis at his mother's funeral

Gladys's death was to be another turning point in the life and career of Elvis Presley. The weirdo with the wiggle who was threatening the whole fabric of the Western World was seen for what he really was. . . an ordinary kid, with ordinary feelings, who loved his country, and above all, loved his mother. The kind of kid any parents would be proud of. It was ironic that the moment of his greatest grief was also the moment of his greatest triumph.

Elvis returned gratefully to his base in Fort Hood, which with its protective routine, provided a cacoon of relative anonymity. He threw himself into his work, trying to prove himself one of the guys, asking nothing, taking nothing and gradually being accepted for what he was – just another GI Joe. He even joined in the celebrations of the country boys when it was announced that his unit would spend the remaining 18 months on active service in Germany.

On 22 September 1958, Elvis, dressed in khaki and carrying a duffel bag over his shoulder, climbed the gangplank of the troop ship *USS General Randall* – as a military band played *Hound Dog* and *All Shook Up*. At a press conference before embarkation, Elvis spoke of his hopes and fears. He said that before he had been drafted he had been hoping to arrange a European tour. "Now I'll get to Europe anyway. I'm looking forward to my first furlough in Paris. I'd like to meet Brigitte Bardot," he joked. Asked if the other soldiers had given him a hard time, he replied, "No sir, I was very surprised. I have never met a nicer group of boys in my life. They probably would have given me a hard time if it had been like everybody thought, that I wouldn't work and I'd be given special treatment". Another reporter asked him what he would do if rock 'n' roll died while he was overseas. He replied "Starve." More seriously, he said that he did not think it would. But if it did. . . "I'd make a serious try to get to the top in movies – that would be my best chance."

It was on the trip over to Bremerhaven that Elvis met up again with a gospel singer and musician called Charlie Hodge. Elvis and Charlie had first met when they both appeared on the Red Foley Show and talked for hours about their mutual friends in showbusiness.

Elvis arranged for Charlie to have the bunk below his on the ship and at nights Charlie could hear Elvis crying in his sleep as he grieved for his mother. Charlie, a natural comedian, made a vow as he listened to Elvis weeping in the darkness. He promised to keep Elvis laughing for the rest of the voyage. He was to do better than that. He was to keep Elvis smiling for the rest of his life. Charlie was still with Elvis when he died.

Elvis rented a house in Bad Nauheim near his base at Freidberg and sent for his father, grandmother, Minnie Mae, and friends Red West and Lamar Fike to join him from Memphis. He would commute to the base every day in a white BMW sports car. He did his duties conscienciously and enthusiastically without ever displaying any great love for Army life. A duty rather than a calling. He was considered to be an above average soldier and was promoted to sergeant and put in charge of a three-man reconnaissance team.

The evenings, Elvis would spend with Red and Lamar and Charlie and a few girls. They would sit around telling jokes, playing the piano and singing. It was at one of these informal get-togethers that Elvis was introduced to a beautiful 14-year-old step daughter of a US Air Force Colonel. . . Priscilla Beaulieu. He met her six weeks before he was due to be demobbed. Elvis was bowled over – not just by her beauty but because she was *not* bowled over by the fact that he was Elvis Presley. And it had been a long time since anyone had reacted like that.

It was announced that Elvis would be demobbed in Early March 1960. He had served his country with credit and without complaint.

> **THE ELVIS DIARY**
> **20 January 1960**
> *Elvis promoted to sergeant.*
>
> **5 March 1960**
> *Elvis is discharged from the Army.*
>
> **20 March 1960**
> *After a triumphant homecoming at Graceland, Elvis goes to the RCA studios in Nashville and records* Soldier Boy *and* Stuck On You. *The single shoots straight to the top of the charts.*

"There was a fierce loyalty that the other guys in the unit had for him and I think it was because they sensed he was a regular guy. He sat in the snow with them, ate the lousy food and the fact that he lived off the post and commuted in a fancy car didn't bother them. . . He would always get a lot of packages filled with cake and candy, more than he could eat, and he'd give it away. The other soldiers thought a lot of him."

An Army spokesman

Chapter Seven

ELVIS GOES TO HOLLYWOOD

◆

Even when the Beatles were at the peak of their popularity in America, a poll was organized asking who the fans preferred – Elvis or the Beatles, and without a No. 1 hit for years Elvis still won the poll by about ten to one.

ABOVE:
Love Me Tender.

THE ELVIS DIARY

March 1960
Elvis's only visit to Britain was at Prestwick Airport, in transit from Germany.

26 April 1960
Elvis returns to Hollywood to begin his first film in two years, G.I. Blues, *co-starring Juliet Prowse.*

8 August 1960
Elvis has his first non-musical film role in Flaming Star, *made for 20th Century-Fox.*

November 1960
Elvis makes his last film for 20th Century-Fox, Wild in the Country, *with Hope Lange.*

April 1961
Elvis begins work on Blue Hawaii, *co-starring Joan Blackman and Angela Lansbury.*

Elvis Presley's post-Army Hollywood career is a lasting tribute to his mystique, his magical appeal, his talent and his greatness. For nobody else but Elvis could have survived the millstones of mediocrity that his later films became.

Elvis returned home to the United States to a welcome once reserved for all-conquering Roman Emperors. He was hailed a King, but it was an empire that he ruled. During his two-year exile his only serious rivals – Buddy Holly, Eddie Cochran, Chuck Berry, Jerry Lee Lewis, Little Richard, Bill Haley, Carl Perkins – had been decimated by death, disgrace and disinterest. Thus Elvis came home to reclaim a crown no-one had been big enough to try for size.

After a two-week rest, he headed for the RCA Victor studios in Nashville for his first civvy street recording session. It was to provide the tracks for his LP *Elvis is Back.* The single chosen to spearhead the Presley revival was *Stuck On You,* but Elvis could have recorded farmyard noises, for all the fans cared. Even before he opened his mouth advance sales had reached 1,275,000. The single went on to sell more than 2 million copies.

But even that was to be outdone by his next two releases. *It's Now or Never* was No.1 in Britain for five weeks and the follow-up, *Are You Lonesome Tonight?,* did even better, with six weeks at the top in November and December of the same year. Elvis was Back. But was he? Presley purists, hankering after the days of *Heartbreak Hotel, Blue Suede Shoes* and *Jailhouse Rock,* were now confronted and confused by a different Elvis to the one they had known before. It seemed that the Army had not only chopped off his sideburns but chopped off his balls as well. Where was the rocker, the rebel, the rockabilly? All they saw was respectability, and their fears were heightened when they tuned in in their millions to watch him appear on television with the arch enemy of rock 'n' roll, Frank Sinatra. Sinatra had denounced rock 'n' roll as phoney and false and claimed it was played and sung by cretinous goons, but his show was slipping in the ratings and he agreed to pay Elvis $125,000 to revive its popularity.

The audience was packed with middle-aged matrons who had forgotten they used to swoon as bobby-soxers for Sinatra. Elvis was ordered not to swing his hips and to wear a dinner jacket. It might just as well have been a strait-jacket – Elvis did little more

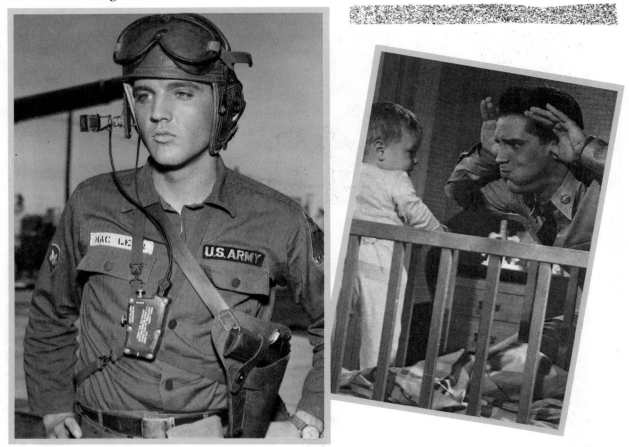

ABOVE LEFT AND RIGHT: *In G.I.Blues*

OPPOSITE: *A brawl scene in* **Blue Hawaii.**

than shake his shoulders. The two superstars sang a bizarre duet in which Elvis sang *Witchcraft* and Sinatra sang *Love Me Tender*.

If the Sinatra Show heightened the fears of the purists, then Elvis's first post-Army movie, *G.I. Blues,* confirmed them. It featured Elvis – his hair dyed black for the first time – as a GI who forms a group to make money to open a night club when they are demobbed. It was a fun film for all the family with lots of children, lots of girls and lots of songs. It made lots and lots of money, grossing more than 4 million dollars in the United States and Canada alone. Commercially it was a great success and financially it provided Elvis with the money to do what he wanted.

His next film was *Flaming Star,* in which he played a half-breed Indian torn between his roots and his upbringing during an uprising. It was a dramatic role – originally written for Marlon Brando – and gave Elvis the opportunity to prove once again that he could act.

Before *Flaming Star* was released he had already started work on his third post-Army film, *Wild in the Country.* Again, it was a dramatic role with Elvis cast in a part that mirrored his early image of delinquent and rebel. It was poorly scripted but the critics agreed that Elvis's performance had saved the film.

As far as the critics were concerned Elvis Presley was set for a career as a serious actor. But – as had always been the case with Elvis – the critics were wrong. Although both films made money, they made nothing like *G.I. Blues.* It seemed that Elvis's legion of new fans – middle-class, middle-aged, middle America – wanted Elvis to sing on screen. And if that was what the paying public wanted, Colonel Parker would make sure that that was what they got.

Elvis's next film, *Blue Hawaii,* set the seal on him in celluloid. It was packed with songs – and good songs – like the title tune, *Hawaiian Wedding Song* and *Can't Help Falling in Love* and *Rock-A-Hula Baby.* Financially it was the biggest success of his film career and the LP alone sold 6 million copies.

Since the Army, Elvis had now released two musicals and two dramas. It was obvious which type of film was making the big money, and it was obvious which direction Elvis's career would take. In February and March of 1961 he had made what was to be the last of his live performances for eight years. Colonel Parker did not want Elvis competing with himself so he kept him clear of television. A producer who called the Colonel and asked what Elvis would want for a walk-on part in a TV show, was given the

THE ELVIS DIARY
July 1961
Elvis starts working on Follow That Dream *– a comedy shot on location in Florida.*

October 1961
Another film for Elvis – Kid Galahad, *with Gig Young and Bronson.*

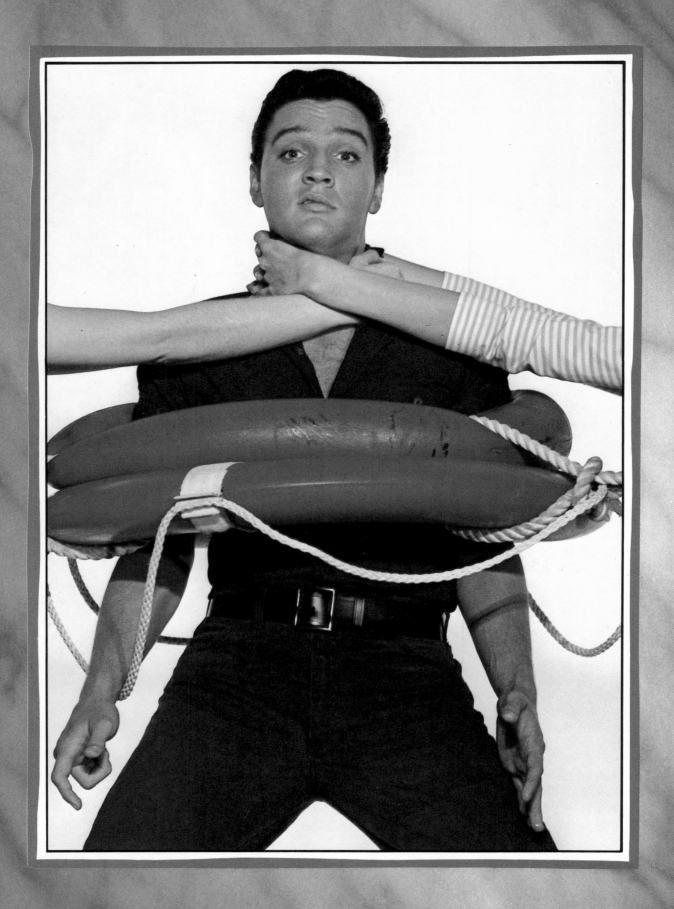

figure of $5,000. The producer could not believe his luck and asked why Elvis was so cheap. The Colonel told him, "Because Elvis will want another 95,000 dollars to walk off again."

Elvis virtually stopped recording as well, apart from the soundtracks of his movie songs. There were occasional sessions at which he recorded songs like *Good Luck Charm, His Latest Flame* and *Little Sister.* These were added to the film songs albums to add a little weight.

From the summer of 1963 – when Elvis reached No.1 in Britain and No.3 in the States with *Devil in Disguise* – until the summer of 1969, when he had a huge hit with *In the Ghetto,* Elvis rarely made the Top Twenty on either side of the Atlantic. The one exception was *Crying in the Chapel,* which, again, reached No.1 in Britain and 3 in the States. It was a recording that Elvis had made in 1960 and had nothing to do with his films, but the lesson went unlearned. The fans were ready to buy anything decent Elvis recorded, but nevertheless he stuck to his film songs.

And if the sole object of Elvis's career was to make money, who was to say he was wrong? Elvis was being paid one million dollars for every film. Plus he got 50 per cent of the profits and all the

OPPOSITE:
Girls! Girls! Girls!

ABOVE:
Fun In Acapulco.

PREVIOUS PAGE:
Roustabout.

ABOVE LEFT AND RIGHT:
Roustabout.

royalties on record sales from the film. Not one of his movies ever lost money. One director commented, "There are only two sure-fire things in this business – Walt Disney and Elvis Presley." The comparison with Walt Disney is intriguing because many people felt that that was what Elvis had become – fantasy entertainment for kids who felt they were too grown-up for cartoons. Too old for the Peter Pan of Walt Disney, they turned to the Peter Pan of Elvis Presley. Like Disney films, Elvis's movies were timed to coincide with school holidays with release dates at Easter, the summer and at Christmas.

Perhaps Colonel Parker reasoned that all Elvis's early fans were now harassed young mothers and that the only way they could get to the cinema to see Elvis on screen would be to take the kids with them. Not only did you get the mums, you got the kids as well – and a new generation of fans. Colonel Parker estimated that there were at least three-quarters of a million Presley fanatics who would pay to see each Elvis film at least three times.

During this period, Elvis not only withdrew from the stage, the TV screen and the recording studio, he also seemed to withdraw from life. He spent the time when he was not filming closeted

LEFT: *With Colonel Parker and Nancy Sinatra off the set of* **Speedway**.

THE ELVIS DIARY

March 1962
Elvis records a single and an album in Nashville, then returns to Hollywood to start work on Girls! Girls! Girls!

May 1962
Priscilla Beaulieu becomes a permanent resident at Graceland.

November 1962
In Hollywood again, Elvis records 10 songs for his next picture, It Happened at the World's Fair.

January 1963
Elvis records 11 new songs for Fun in Acapulco, *his first film of the year.*

May 1963
Elvis returns to Nashville and records 14 songs, of which Devil in Disguise *is chosen to be a single, and is an instant success.*

August 1963
Work begins on Viva Las Vegas, *co-starring Ann-Margret.*

October 1963
Elvis's third film of the year, Kissin' Cousins, *made for MGM.*

away behind the gates of Graceland, cossetted by his own Imperial Guard living a life as unreal as it was unrewarding. Not even the phenomenal success of the Beatles seemed able to shake him out of his personal and professional torpor. Not even when the Beatles broke his own record for viewers on the Ed Sullivan Show was Elvis goaded into life.

The Beatles confessed that there was only one person they really wanted to meet in America – and that was Elvis Presley. They freely admitted that Elvis had been the biggest influence on their careers and John Lennon said, "Before Elvis there was nothing. Without Elvis there would be no Beatles." A meeting was arranged between Elvis and the Fab Four at which they were awestruck. Elvis broke the ice and the five got on famously and even got together for a brief jam session – a tape of which would be worth a fortune if it ever existed.

John Lennon, the most outspoken of the Beatles, asked Elvis why he was no longer making decent records. Elvis mumbled something about hectic film schedules and said that one day he might make some of his old style records again. John Lennon said, "We'll buy it."

OPPOSITE: *Publicity shot for*
King Creole.

Elvis being **Girl Happy.**

ABOVE: *With Joan Blackman in **Blue Hawaii.***

THE ELVIS DIARY

March 1964
Elvis starts working on Roustabout *with Barbara Stanwyck and Joan Freeman.*

July 1964
Filming begins on Girl Happy, *co-starring Shelley Fabares.*

21 October 1964
Elvis makes Tickle Me, *with Julie Adams and Jocelyn Lane. Although disliked by the critics, the film made a healthy profit for United Artists.*

February 1965
Elvis begins filming Harum Scarum.

May 1965
Elvis makes Frankie and Johnny *for United Artists, with Nancy Novack and Donna Douglas.*

Even when the Beatles were at the peak of their popularity in America, a poll was organized asking who the fans preferred – Elvis or the Beatles, and without a No.1 hit for years, Elvis still won the poll by about ten to one, suggesting that perhaps Beatles fans had no money for postage because they were spending it all on records and that Elvis fans could afford the postage because they had no records to buy.

Elvis even stopped giving press interviews. . . on the grounds that giving an interview to one newspaper would make enemies of all the other newspapers. Elvis was now so exclusive, he was in danger of becoming totally excluded. Only one event in the middle 1960s aroused any real interest in Elvis. . . his marriage to Priscilla Beaulieu at Las Vegas in 1967.

Priscilla had gone to live at Graceland with Vernon Presley and his second wife, Dee. It was part of a deal Elvis had struck with Priscilla's father after he had met her in Germany. Elvis appears to have seen something in her that he wanted to preserve and mould. While she lived at Graceland under the supervision of Dee and Vernon, she attended an all girls' high school and never dated boys. When Elvis was not filming he would return to Graceland and continue the grooming of the girl everyone assumed would one day be his bride. He told her how to wear her hair, told her to dye it black, told her how to do her eyes, and while Priscilla served her "apprenticeship" Elvis continued to sow his wild oats out in Hollywood with a succession of starlets. When asked why he had never married, Elvis replied, in an untypically unguarded moment, "Why buy apples when you live in an orchard?" And as the Press picked up on his latest affair Priscilla would try to ape his newest love. When he was dating Ann-Margret heavily, Priscilla started dance lessons and even wore her hair like Ann.

But Elvis was now 32 and, Priscilla made it clear she was not going to wait for ever. The Colonel weighed up the situation. Perhaps Elvis would lose a lot of fans if he married – but maybe not as many as he would gain with the added respectability and acceptability marriage and a family would give him. The Colonel gave them his blessing.

Elvis married Priscilla on the morning of 1 May 1967 – three weeks before her 22nd birthday – and, like everything about Elvis at this time, the event was shrouded in secrecy. Rumours were rife

that Elvis and Priscilla were about to marry but as they were on holiday in Palm Springs everyone assumed that that was where the ceremony would take place, but in the early hours of 1 May, Elvis and Priscilla flew into Las Vegas and immediately headed for the Clark County courthouse where they took out a special licence for $15. They then drove to the Aladdin Hotel where they were married by Judge David Zenoff, a justice of the Nevada Supreme Court, in the manager's private suite. The ceremony lasted only eight minutes and Priscilla – her black hair piled high on top of her head – wore a white chiffon gown with a 6-foot train, and a three-carat diamond ring surrounded by a cluster of 20 smaller diamonds. Elvis wore a black tuxedo and Priscilla promised to love, honour, cherish and comfort him. She did not promise to obey him – and perhaps it was an omen for their turbulent future.

A press conference was called of all the reporters and photographers who had converged on Las Vegas expecting an announcement of Elvis's wedding. They got what they wanted – but not what they had expected. The wedding had already taken place. Elvis was already married.

"She was one of the few girls who was interested in me for me alone."
Elvis on Priscilla

ABOVE LEFT:
Fun In Acapulco.

ABOVE RIGHT: *With Ann-Margret in* **Viva Las Vegas.**

THE ELVIS DIARY

July 1965
Elvis makes Paradise Hawaiian Style *for Paramount.*

27 August 1965
Elvis meets The Beatles at his house on Perugia Way, Beverly Hills. No photos or recording were allowed under Elvis's instructions.

February 1966
Elvis makes his sixth picture for MGM, Spinout.

June 1966
Elvis's next picture, Double Trouble.

September 1966
Easy Come, Easy Go – *a film made for Hal Wallis.*

OPPOSITE:
Viva Las Vegas.

LEFT: *The wedding.*

By now, the Hollywood years had taken a heavy toll on Elvis – not only on his popularity but also his health. In between films he had taken to going on eating binges and his weight ballooned. To counter this and also to enable himself to stay up late at parties and stay fresh for the day's work, he started taking diet pills. Then, after taking uppers he would need downers so that he could get to sleep. It was a cycle that began in Hollywood and was born of boredom – and one that Elvis was never really able to break.

Elvis was now so nauseated by his films that they literally made him physically sick. Then, because of production difficulties, one film was shot in two weeks, and this set the pattern for the rest of his career in films – a shorter production schedule meant even greater profits. Now even a conscientious professional like Elvis could no longer pretend to take the movies seriously.

He had one last stab at serious acting as a gunslinger in *Charro* in which the only song he sings is in the opening credits. But by now Elvis Presley films were so devalued – often featuring as support films – that many critics did not even bother to review it.

Nine months after his marriage, Priscilla presented Elvis with a baby daughter, Lisa Marie, and perhaps for the first time for years, Elvis could see some purpose to this life, some future. However, there was an emptiness inside him that even his family could not fulfil, but there was another family that could. . . his fans. Elvis called Colonel Parker and told him bluntly not to sign any more film contracts. "If you do, I will not turn up on the set," he told the Colonel. And he added the words his fans had been waiting seven long years to hear: "I'm going back on the road."

THE ELVIS DIARY

8 February 1967
Elvis buys himself a 163-acre ranch in DeSoto County, and names it Circle G ranch. Here he will spend many happy days relaxing and riding in privacy.

February 1967
Elvis makes a short trip to Nashville to record the tunes for Clambake *before returning to Hollywood to make the film.*

1 May 1967
Elvis (32) and Priscilla (21) are married in Las Vegas. After a brief press conference and a small reception, the couple honeymoon in Palm Springs.

June 1967
Elvis starts work on Speedway, *co-starring Nancy Sinatra.*

18 October 1967
The start of work on Stay Away, Joe *a comedy picture made for MGM.*

1 February 1968
A daughter, Lisa Marie, is born to Elvis and Priscilla. They are bombarded with cards and gifts from well-wishers all over the world.

March 1968
Elvis returns to Hollywood to work on his next film, Live A Little, Love A Little.

Chapter Eight

THE
'COMEBACK'

◆

"The pop world has changed overnight with the reappearance of the man they call The King. Mark my words... he is going to be immense all over again." *A critic*

THE ELVIS DIARY

22 July 1968
Elvis stars in another non-musical film, Charro. *He plays a "Clint Eastwood" part.*

October 1968
Elvis starts work on The Trouble With Girls *– an MGM picture.*

3 December 1968
Elvis is seen on television in an NBC TV Special, which becomes known as "The Comeback". The critics are ecstatic. New Musical Express *in Britain vote him "Best Vocalist of the Year".*

OPPOSITE: *The NBC TV special.*

He paced the small make-up room, tucked away at the back of the NBC studios. Only minutes to go. Just moments until he came face to face with destiny or destruction. He was a panther, prowling, covered head to foot in glossy black leather, sleek, powerful, fierce – frightened. Little beads of sweat broke through the heavy stage make-up. He wrung his hands, then clenched one fist, smashing it into the palm of his other hand.

Elvis Presley had been locked away for nearly eight years. Caged, controlled, contained, restrained, and now was about to be let loose on an audience. But he wasn't sure that the flock of faithful outside in the TV studio wouldn't turn on him and tear him apart. Not physically and in worship as they had done ten long years ago, but critically and with ridicule.

As his stomach churned and his hands trembled, Elvis wondered if the critics were right. Was he merely a relic of an age long passed? Was his career really dead and buried under the rubble of more than two dozen films? Could he still work an audience? Could Elvis Presley still cut it? In barely more than a whisper, talking more to himself than to the few close friends who shared the small room and his fears, he said, "I haven't been in front of these people in years. What if they don't like me? What if they laugh at me?"

A voice sounded from outside the door. It cut through the room like an invitation to mount the gallows. "Mr Presley. . . you're on."

Elvis shook visibly, his hands quivering uncontrollably. He wove his way through the back of the studio, closer, closer to the stage. He was deaf to the music, deaf to the good wishes of his friends, deaf to the expectant hum of his fans. Deaf to all but the pounding of his heart.

As Elvis walked on stage the audience rose as one, cheering, chanting, clapping. He reached for the microphone. The fans saw the shaking hand and loved him for his humility. The microphone was in his fist, the song was in his heart. . . and the audience was in the palm of his hand. It was as if Elvis Presley, the man, the mere mortal, had been left behind back-stage. And the Elvis Presley who walked out on stage was the legend, the myth, the deity. The audience went wild. Elvis Presley was back on stage, back on top, back on Olympus. Elvis Presley was Back.

The way back home for Elvis had been tortuous, littered with torment, challenge and self-doubt and the burning realization that he could lose what he held most dear – his self-respect. That had begun to happen anyway through his movies, but to have been rejected by an audience would have been too hard to bear.

Marriage and fatherhood – Lisa Marie had been born exactly nine months after their wedding day – had changed Elvis. As he held his tiny child, he realized that he could no longer play the boy-man character that typified so many of his films. But more than Priscilla, more than Lisa Marie, there was another reason that forced Elvis to change the direction of his flagging career – namely that, to all but his most loyal fans – and they were still counted in their hundreds of thousands – Elvis had become a joke. He was being laughed at. To admit to being an Elvis fan was to invite ridicule. How much worse was it for Elvis?

If there was one thing Elvis Presley could not live without, it was being Elvis Presley – and all that meant. He knew his crown was not only slipping, but in danger of falling off. Elvis knew he could end up a forgotten man – a man assured of a place in history, but with no place guaranteed in the charts.

Steve Binder, the producer of the NBC Singer Special TV comeback, had done more than most to persuade Elvis to face facts. Elvis had complained that he could go nowhere, do nothing without being mobbed by fans. Binder challenged Elvis to put it to the test – and stand on Sunset Strip in the middle of the day. Elvis did just that – and went unrecognized. It meant one of two things. Either Elvis was not the magnet he once had been or he had been a recluse for so long that people did not expect to see him on a public highway and believed it must be one of his many look-alikes. Either way Elvis was forced to face the truth – out of sight had been out of mind.

In January 1968 Colonel Parker announced that NBC and Singer sewing machines were financing an Elvis TV Special, to be broadcast at Christmas. The fee was to be $500,000 – a figure so high that few could even believe it was credible. Only Colonel Parker would have demanded it. Only Elvis Presley could have commanded it.

Legend has it that Colonel Parker wanted Elvis to do a Perry Como-style Christmas show, along the lines of his films, with Elvis coming out and singing a handful of mushy, sentimental, seasonal

Charro!

Change of Habit with Mary Tyler Moore.

songs and, at the end, waving and saying "Merry Christmas – and goodnight everybody." Elvis and Steve Binder were horrified. They knew that if he did that it would be "Merry Christmas – and goodnight Elvis." It seems more likely that the Colonel – who never interfered with the musical direction of Elvis's career – was trying to goad Elvis and Steve into making the Singer Special something very special.

If that was his aim, then he certainly succeeded. As Elvis walked out on stage at the NBC studio on the night of 27 June 1968, for the taping of the first of four shows before a live audience, he looked better than he had since the late 1950s. He had slimmed down and lost the chubby, well-fed, contented look of some of his later films. He had grown his sideburns and was dressed in black leather. The rebel had been reborn.

At the end he sang a song, specially written for him, called *If I Can Dream*. It was to become Elvis's first real hit for three years, making the Top Twenty in both America and Great Britain.

The show was a spectacular success, topping the ratings in America. The fans went wild. So did the critics. One wrote, "There is something magical about watching a man who has lost himself

TOP: ***The Trouble with Girls.***

RIGHT: *Signing autographs.*

ABOVE: *Coming on stage in Las Vegas.*

OPPOSITE: *Leaving Graceland.*

find his way back home." Elvis was indeed on his way back home. But not quite there. He still had a Hollywood contract and more films to make. But by now he knew where he was going. He said, "I'm planning a lot of changes because you cannot go on doing the same thing year after year and it has been a long time since I have done anything professionally except make movies and cut albums. From now on I don't think I'd like to do so many pictures and I have been doing almost three a year. . . Before too long I'm going to make some personal appearance tours, probably starting here in this country and then play some concerts abroad. I want to see some places I've never seen before. I miss the personal contact with audiences."

But first he had a Hollywood contract to honour. His next film was *Charro,* a totally different kind of part for Elvis in which he played a gunslinger. There was only one song, sung over the credits, and his performance had many people talking about an Oscar for Elvis. It was another step in the right direction – but an even more significant step had already been taken. Elvis had recorded some new material.

On 13 January 1969, Elvis arrived at the American Sound Studio in Memphis to record in his home town for the first time since 1956. That session lasted until 23 January. Another followed from 17 February and lasted until 22 February. Backed by the best session musicians in Memphis, all major talents in their own right and brought up on and with the same feel for the mix of gospel, soul, blues, and rock 'n' roll, Elvis put together some of the best material of his life. In all, 35 tracks were recorded. Of those, *In the Ghetto* and *Suspicious Minds* were smash hits and two others, *Don't Cry Daddy* and *Kentucky Rain,* were both Top Twenty hits. The rest of the material formed two albums – *From Elvis in Memphis* and the second half of the double LP *Elvis – From Memphis to Vegas/From Vegas to Memphis.*

Elvis's career had now been rejuvenated, re-shaped and reborn. Only one thing was missing – his return to live performances. As he was putting to rest his old image with the completion of his last two films *The Trouble With Girls And How to Get Into It* and *Change of Habit,* it was announced that there was truly *going* to be a change of habit for Elvis Presley. Colonel Parker made it public that Elvis was starting rehearsals for the first of his live shows in Las Vegas on 31 July. The transition from Memphis recluse to megastar was about to be completed.

The scene for Elvis's comeback was to be the International Hotel, Las Vegas, the biggest and most luxurious hotel even Vegas had ever seen. It had more than 1,500 rooms, cost more than $60 million to build, stood 30 storeys high and its swimming-pool was the largest stretch of water in Nevada apart from Lake Mead. The main showroom had a seating capacity of 2,000. It was the biggest ever and it wanted the best ever. Elvis set himself one standard – which was to be the guideline for his future – when he set about planning the Vegas show, "I don't care if I don't make any money as long as I give them a good show."

In the early stages of planning the comeback, Colonel Parker had thought of a number of huge venues throughout the United States which could accommodate thousands of people, but the International Hotel was offering enough money to satisfy even the Colonel... $1 million for a month-long season. There was another attraction about Vegas – it was a resort and people came from all over the world to enjoy the gambling casinos and entertainment. This meant that some of Elvis's foreign fans would get to see him.

However after his disaster at Las Vegas at the Frontier Hotel in 1956, when the Colonel had to cancel the second week of a concert because of poor response, Elvis had reservations about the town. In 1956 the Colonel had vowed never to bring Elvis back to Vegas until they paid him the highest fee a star had ever been paid. Now, the International Hotel quickly overcame the Colonel's reservations.

Tom Jones helped Elvis overcome *his*. Elvis and Priscilla flew into Vegas to watch Tom perform. Elvis was knocked out at the response to the Welsh singer from his largely middle-aged female audience. Their reactions of near hysteria reminded Elvis of the response to him back in the 1950s. He watched how Tom wound up the audience by mopping his brow with a handkerchief and then passing the handkerchief down to an adoring female. After the show he talked to Tom and the two swopped notes.

By now, Elvis liked the whole atmosphere of Vegas, the style, the sophistication, the sheer scale of everything. At last he was convinced that Vegas was right. But what he *didn't* want was to appear on stage in a tuxedo. He was already working on a dance routine, trying to incorporate karate moves, so he commissioned designer Bill Belew to create a suit based on the traditional karate outfit.

Elvis then brought together the best musicians money could buy and flew out to Los Angeles to begin the early stages of rehearsing – starting with more than 100 songs and gradually whittling them down to a handful. The next stage – two weeks before opening – was full rehearsals, with his vocal backing groups, the Imperials and the Sweet Inspirations, and the hotel's 25-piece orchestra. As soon as it was announced that Elvis was to appear at the International the hotel switchboard was jammed with callers from all over the world begging for tickets.

Throughout the final two weeks Elvis had been demanding but understanding, gently encouraging more from his musicians, ruthlessly forcing even more from himself. They grew to love him. What they gave would come from the heart; what Elvis gave would come from the soul.

On the night of 31 July 1969, Elvis was experiencing the same fears and self-doubts he had suffered a year before on the first night of the Singer TV Special. He had less reason with the success of the previous 12 months, but still there were doubts. They lasted

THE ELVIS DIARY

31 July 1969
Elvis's first night at the international Hotel's "Showroom Internationale". He receives 1 million dollars for his four-week engagement. The music critics are unanimous in their praise.

4 November 1969
The single Suspicious Minds *reaches No. 1 in the American charts.* Don't Cry Daddy *follows this success, soon reaching No. 6.*

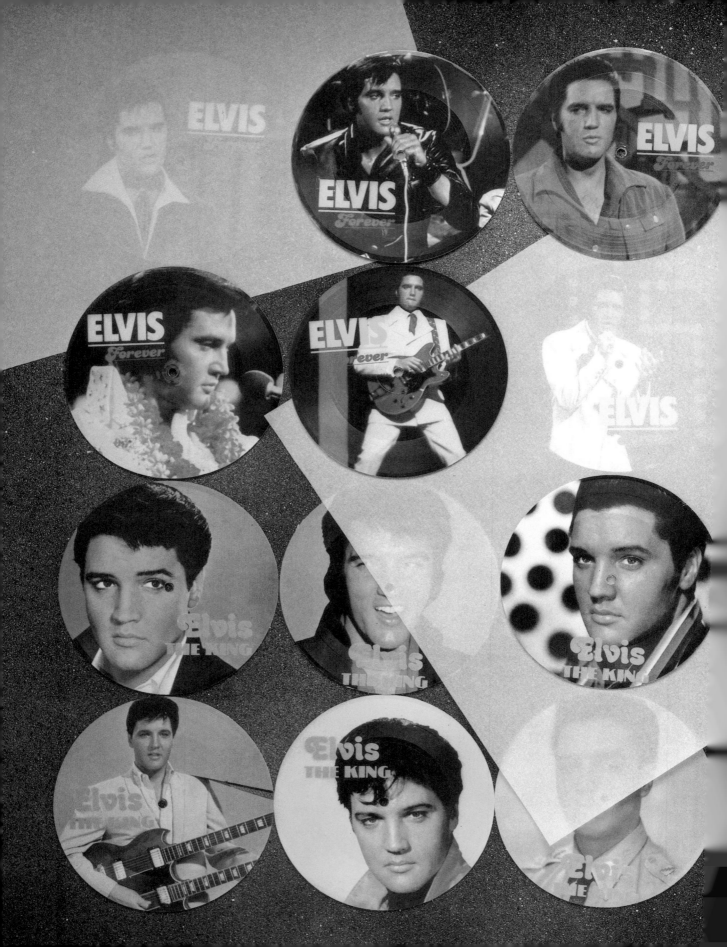

for the immeasurable amount of time it takes for a man to walk on stage, for an audience to get to its feet and for a roar of gratitude and adulation to erupt from 2,000 throats.

His act took him through 13 years of hits, evoking memories, provoking emotions. He started with *Blue Suede Shoes,* went into *I Got A Woman,* reduced the women to trembling adoration with *Love Me Tender.* Then he reminded the audience that he was not just a ghostly figure from the past, but a tangible presence for the future as he sang, first, his recent *In The Ghetto* and then the about-to-be-released *Suspicious Minds.*

He was a sensation.

"The pop world has changed overnight with the reappearance of the man they call The King. Mark my words. . . he is going to be immense all over again."   *A critic*

The critic from *Newsweek* said, "There are several unbelievable things about Elvis but the most incredible is his staying power in a world where meteoric careers fade like shooting stars."

At a press conference afterwards Elvis was asked why he had left it so long before returning to live performances. He replied, "I have always wanted to perform on the stage again for the last nine years. It has been building up inside of me since 1965 until the strain became intolerable. I don't think I could have taken it much longer." He also said he would be less than honest if he did not admit, he was ashamed of some of the movies and songs he had done. "I got more pleasure out of performing to an audience like tonight than any of the film songs have given me."

In the four weeks that Elvis appeared at the International Hotel he had outdrawn Frank Sinatra, Dean Martin and Barbra Streisand. A total of 101,500 people had been to see him. Not one seat remained unsold. It is a record that still stands.

By the end of the month people were no longer talking about the Elvis comeback. It was as if he had never been away.

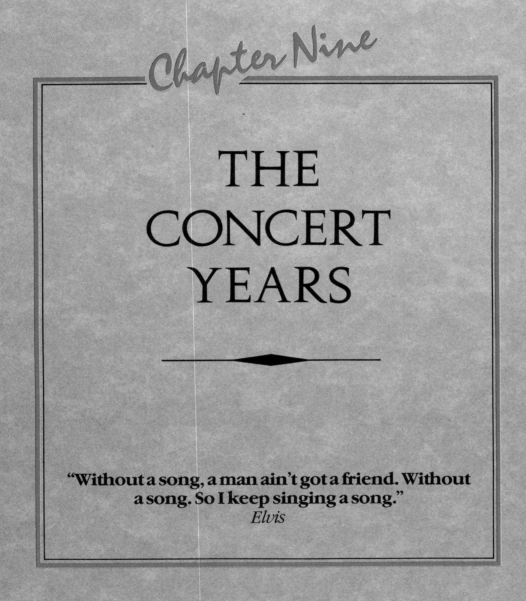

Chapter Nine

THE CONCERT YEARS

◆

"Without a song, a man ain't got a friend. Without a song. So I keep singing a song."
Elvis

THE ELVIS DIARY

28 February 1970
Elvis flies to Houston to play six concerts in The Astrodome, nicknamed "The eighth wonder of the world".

6 July 1970
The start of filming of Elvis: That's The Way It Is – a film made by MGM of Elvis – from rehearsal to final performance.

21 December 1970
Elvis meets President Nixon.

Only one performer in history has matched the success, popularity and appeal of the Elvis Presley of the late 1950s and early 1960s – the Elvis Presley of the late 1960s and early 1970s. But those to whom the gods grant great gifts must pay a savage price, and Elvis Presley was no exception.

Perhaps there are gods who give and gods who take away. Perhaps the gods who give are the same gods who also take away, to remind their chosen few that they are, after all, merely mortal.

At the pinnacle of his first career, Elvis was to suffer the loss of everything he had lived for. . . his beloved mother. Elvis died believing that if he had not been Elvis Presley then his mother would have lived. Gladys could not live with his success, his marriage could not survive his success. And Elvis never truly survived the failure of his marriage.

If his first loss had marked the beginning of the end of an era in his career, the second loss was to mark the beginning of the end of an era. . .

The critics said it was too soon. The cynics hoped it really was. Elvis Presley announced that he would return to the stage of the International Hotel, Las Vegas – just six months after his comeback show.

The critics and the cynics. . . he knocked them sideways. The fans. . . he knocked them dead. A week before the two-month engagement began, every seat was sold. He opened on 24 January 1970 – the beginning of a third decade of domination. His act had changed – there was less emphasis on the past, more on the future. Less of what once had been, more of what was to come. Instead of singing only his own hits, Elvis now introduced other songs that had been successes for other artists, and made them his own. . . classics like *Proud Mary, Walk A Mile In My Shoes* and *Polk Salad Annie.*

As before at the International, RCA recorded Elvis live and the album, *Elvis – On Stage,* sold one million copies. Elvis also introduced another million seller at this series of concerts – *Kentucky Rain.*

Elvis was now as big – or even bigger – than he had ever been. After one of the shows Sammy Davis Jr offered this explanation of the phenomenon called Elvis Presley: "When he comes on stage he is just special. I love Elvis on stage. I admire him as a friend. I

honour his friendship and I think he is just a groovy down-to-earth cat, someone who does it better than anybody else – because he invented it."

It was not just the repertoire that had changed. Elvis had grown his hair so that it covered his ears. He looked better for putting on a little weight and he had lost that gaunt, haunted, half-starved look of the year before.

He had by now developed his jokey, folksey style of talking to the audience between songs, dodging the cascade of bras, lace panties and room keys that showered the stage. One night he teased the audience about his "shaky leg". "One day I went to Disneyland and three kids got on my leg and tried to ride me. Before I could tell them I wasn't a ride, they'd already popped three quarters in my mouth."

Elvis closed in Las Vegas and after just a couple of days rest flew to Houston, Texas, to star as the big draw at the Livestock Show and Rodeo at the Houston Astrodome. As Elvis told his Las Vegas audience, "I'll be there with the cattle."

There were many reasons why the Houston Astrodome had been chosen for Elvis's first public appearance outside Las Vegas. For a start it held 44,500 people. In the words of the Colonel, "To maintain his image as King, my boy needs super engagements. By appearing in Las Vegas's biggest showroom and in the Astrodome, he has just that." Elvis also wanted to get to the biggest number of people possible in what had been the heartland of his support back in the 1950s. He loved performing in Las Vegas but he knew that his real fans would never have the money to see him there. The Astrodome could accommodate so many people that prices did not have to be high to cover expenses. Some seats for the four evening shows and two matinees sold for as little as a dollar.

The Texans called the Astrodome, with its 1 m.p.h. breeze maintaining a constant temperature of 72°F, the eighth wonder of the world. They quickly renamed it the ninth – they had just seen the eighth on stage.

Elvis was guaranteed $100,000 for every show plus a percentage of the box office. It is said that he picked up a total of more than $1.2 million. He was watched by nearly a quarter of a million people in just six performances.

At this stage in his career, Elvis had finished his movie commitments. His last film, *Change of Habit,* had been released but, with the resurgence of the "live" Elvis, it had been quietly forgotten. But with the phenomenal new success Elvis was enjoying it was as if Hollywood had discovered him all over again. The offers poured in.

But the Colonel and Elvis both knew that any interruptions to make the silly, fluffy films that had so nearly destroyed him before, would steal from the impetus Elvis was now creating as a born-again entertainer.

The Colonel didn't exactly say No. In fact he often said Yes – on certain conditions: $1 million for ten weeks' work, 50 per cent of the profits, 25 per cent of television sales on top of the 10 per cent for distribution. No picture was to cost more than $2 million, no shooting after six at weekends, no shooting during the last two weeks of December to the first weeks of January. And if the picture over-ran its schedule of ten weeks. . . then say goodbye budget, film, Elvis and career. Not surprisingly, when the Colonel said Yes, the producer said No.

But the Colonel did not say Yes in such a negative way to *all* film offers. Sometimes he said Yes – and actually meant it. One such offer was for a documentary film about Elvis shot during rehearsals and shows while he was performing in Las Vegas. It was to be a very different sort of film. For the first time the fans were to be shown what Elvis was like off-stage. The tensions and the nerves he experienced. For the first time they were to be shown that Elvis really did exist, that he was human, that he really did live . . . and not just in their dreams.

Denie Sanders, the director, said, "We attempted to capture the ups and down he experiences putting his show together, showing the man as a musician. We filmed both sides of the lights, exploring what he feels and the emotions he creates in others. Once on stage before an audience, the thing he has as a performer is what Brando had at the height of his powers as an actor. That is, you can never anticipate what he is going to do next. Each of his shows is entirely different. Though he is well prepared, it is instinct that guides him on stage. It is difficult to take your eyes off him. I found it difficult to take the cameras off him and focus on some other aspect of the show."

OPPOSITE: *The Aztec Suit in 1975.*

LEFT: *Elvis at the wedding of Sonny West.*

His assistant director, John Wilson, said, "Elvis is magic. That's the word for it – he just pulls people. Elvis is a real, genuine warm human being, he's friendly, he loves people. And I guess that must be the key to it. The people who are watching in the audience. . . they just feel that."

Elvis – That's The Way It Is, was filmed during rehearsals at MGM Studios, rehearsals in Las Vegas and then on stage at the International. . . the cameras were still there when Elvis opened at Phoenix, Arizona, on 9 September 1970. Elvis had kept faith with his fans. He knew that the Las Vegas prices excluded most of them. If the fans could not come to him, then he would go to them.

Phoenix, Arizona, 9 September 1970 – the opening night of Elvis Presley's first concert tour for 13 long years. The comeback was complete.

From Phoenix it was St Louis, Detroit, Miami, Tampa and Mobile. The fans poured in and so did the plaudits. "Elvis Presley has returned and he is a triumph," screamed one newspaper. "Presley was in command of his performances. Those who went got their money's worth in talent and memories and he is an artist who appreciates his audience."

Another critic wrote, "At 35, Elvis is still youthful and trim, hair jet-black and long. He may shake his head more now than the hip bones but he can still throw a mean bump. An evening with Elvis will make a television viewer realize how much Tom Jones has copied Elvis and the real product is so much better. . . When Elvis got up on the stage it was the 4th of July all over again as thousands of flashbulbs blinked through the hall. The Elvis movements are rhythmic and sure-footed. . . so smooth and sexual they seem spontaneous. The whole evening was a bombastic, one-man triumph and a significant tribute to Presley's quite unusual and magnetic stage appeal."

Elvis took a month off – and then it was back on the road again with an eight-city tour. At the Los Angeles Forum the first show sold out in five hours and to satisfy public demand a matinee performance was hurriedly arranged. That sold out in two days. When Elvis went on stage he looked around the audience and said, with genuine humility, "So this is the audience that sold this place out in five hours. . . thank you. Thank you very much."

In 1971 Elvis began the year with another month-long season at Las Vegas. He was back again for a week in July and then a month in September/August. And then he was on the road again. This time on a 12-city tour. 1971 was a special year in many ways for Elvis. In this year the road that runs past the front of Graceland was renamed Elvis Presley Boulevard, and Elvis was also to be given one of his most treasured awards. In January 1971, dressed in a black mink tuxedo, he was named as one of the 10 Outstanding Young Men in America by the United States Jaycees Auditorium.

Accepting the award, Elvis revealed much of the driving force and philosophy that had guided and directed his life. He said, "I've always been a dreamer. When I was young I read comic books and I was the hero of the comic book. I saw a movie and I was the hero of the movie. So every dream that I ever dreamed has come true a hundred times." Then he pointed to the nine other award winners and added, "These gentlemen here are the type of people who care, who are dedicated. You realize that it is possible that they might build the kingdom of heaven. It is not too far fetched from reality. . . I'd like to say that I learned very early in life that without a song, a day will never end. Without a song, a man ain't got a friend. Without a song. So I keep singing a song."

THE ELVIS DIARY

23 February 1972
Elvis is shattered by Priscilla's announcement in Las Vegas that she is leaving him.

March 1972
Elvis starts work on his last film, Elvis On Tour, a revealing look at the star at work and at play, both on-stage and off.

9 June 1972
Elvis plays Madison Square Gardens in New York.

18 August 1972
Elvis files a law suit in a Santa Monica Divorce Court.

When Elvis was not on tour or appearing at Las Vegas at the Hilton (the renamed International) or the Sahara Tahoe, he would go home – for that is how he always regarded Graceland. For relaxation he and a crowd of friends would head for one of the local cinemas around midnight for an all-night movie session. Elvis would watch anything – he had to. He watched so many films it was either watch anything – or nothing.

He was a movie buff who would watch a favourite film over and over again. He knew James Dean's lines off by heart in the film *Rebel Without A Cause*. And two of his other all-time favourites were *Patton – Lust for Glory,* starring George C. Scott, and *Dr Strangelove,* starring Peter Sellers. He was a great fan of Sellers and loved all the "Pink Panther" films.

During the day Elvis and the Guys would saddle up their horses. Elvis would usually ride Rising Sun and often he would go down to the gates at Graceland to talk to the fans and sign autographs. Graceland had always been a tourist attraction but since Elvis's resurgence it had become a honeypot. The local police were often called out just to control the fans – especially if Elvis had turned up at the gates that day.

At other times he would ride his motorcycle, or golf cart, practise his karate or – perhaps his favourite pastime – read. Elvis would read anything, particularly books with a theme of religion or mysticism. His friends believed he was searching for an answer that he never ever found, could never hope to find, "Why am *I* Elvis Presley?"

1972 again began with Elvis back in Las Vegas and then in April he began another tour – but this time with a difference. Apart from his personal entourage, his band, backing singers, a 12-piece orchestra, a comedian, engineers and technicians, Elvis was accompanied by another team – a film crew.

Elvis was about to make the 33rd – and final – movie of his career. *Elvis On Tour* was just that. It was a tour of Elvis, from his beginnings right through his career up to that current tour.

But his biggest triumph of 1972 he saved for New York. Elvis had never played the Big Apple – the only star ever to attain nationwide success who had not. As soon as the news was announced that Elvis would do a total of six shows at Madison Square Gardens in June of 1972, the queues began to form. The same girls who had nearly rioted at the première of *Love Me*

Tender all those years before, were back again – many with their daughters, a new generation of fans.

Like an artist with an empty canvas, the conductor lifted his baton and with a flick of his wrist made the first stroke of what was to be a masterpiece of presentation. The orchestra burst into the first explosive, soaring notes of the theme from *2001 A Space Odyssey*. Light beams slashed around the huge arena and then as one came together like a great timeless tunnel of light from another galaxy. As the audience caught its breath, there, in that spotlight from the stars, stood the almost ephemeral figure of the man who could have been of another time: Elvis Presley.

He did four shows in three days, every one sold out and the box office take was $750,000, of which Elvis got a third, not to mention royalties from the rush-release LP of the shows that was on sale within three days.

Elvis's success at Madison Square Gardens finally clinched, for Colonel Parker, his biggest and most audacious deal of all time. The Colonel announced that he had arranged the most spectacular concert ever. It would be held at the Honolulu International Centre and would be beamed by satellite throughout the world. *Aloha from Hawaii* was to be watched worldwide by an audience of more than one billion people – more than watched Man's first walk on the moon.

Elvis had not just scaled a peak, ascended an unconquered pinnacle. He had mounted Olympus. The jealous gods looked down at the man who had assumed the aura of immortality. . . And decided it was time he paid.

THE ELVIS DIARY
14 January 1973
Elvis's TV satellite show "Aloha From Hawaii" is watched by 1 billion viewers all over the world.

Chapter Ten

THE FINAL YEARS

◆

"Ladies and Gentlemen ... Elvis has left the building." *Jacky Kahane*

Professionally, Elvis Presley was at the very summit of his success. Personally, he was in the depths of despair.

Priscilla came to him one night in Las Vegas after the two evening shows. He knew it must be serious for her to break the hard and fast "No Wives on Tour" rule. He knew it was not just serious. He knew it was trouble.

He cleared the penthouse of his friends and aides. This was something between just the two of them. He knew someone would be on guard outside the door. There always was — ever since the first of the death threats.

There was a knock at the door. He was about to mumble "Come in" but didn't bother. The door opened as he knew it would. He heard it close. He was sitting with his back to the door, gazing through the vast panoramic windows, down on the pleasure-promising lights of Vegas. He could see Priscilla reflected in the window.

There was something in her manner. Something in her eyes. "Elvis," she said. Her voice was clear, resolute, as if rehearsed. "Elvis," she repeated more firmly. She wanted him to turn round. She wanted to tell him face to face. The figure at the window did not move.

"Elvis, I am leaving you."

Elvis knew then why he had not turned round. No matter how much he had anticipated those words, dreaded them, no matter how much he prepared, no matter how he tried, he knew he would not be able to hide his feelings. He reached down to a table at his side and felt for a pair of shades, and put them on. To mask the tears he felt welling in his eyes.

He could hear Priscilla talking, vague, distant, as if from another room. She had found another man. . . she loved him. . . she was leaving. . .

He heard the door close. Her reflection left the window. She had left the room. She had left his life.

He sat there, gazing down on Vegas, the lights a blur through his tears. Had he said a word? There was so much he could have said. So much he had said over the years. So many promises he had made. So many he had broken. It was too late for promises. Too late for Priscilla.

Where had it all gone wrong? He knew only too well. . .

THE ELVIS DIARY

July 1973
Elvis's ill-health has been noticed and is beginning to cause concern.

25 October 1973
Elvis enters Baptist Memorial Hospital, Memphis, for rest. He leaves on 1 November.

THE ELVIS DIARY
8 January 1974
Elvis learns that Jimmy Carter, the then Governor of Georgia, has appointed this, his birthday, as "Elvis Presley Day".

Since the age of 15 Priscilla had been as much a prisoner of Elvis as Elvis had been of his fans. His way of life had been her way of life. Graceland had been a gilded cage – as much a prison as a palace. At first there had been time together, but when Elvis went back to performing live, there had been little.

For six months of any year she had been alone. Wives were banned on tour. She never asked why – she knew. Elvis Presley was the world's most desirable man. He had made the most of that as a single man and she had no doubt that marriage had brought no change.

Perhaps even that might have been bearable, but even when he was at home, they shared little time together, especially alone. Priscilla was a lark; Elvis was an owl. Elvis would rise late and come to bed just as Priscilla was about to get up to go to a dance class or a karate class. Even the hours they shared awake, they rarely shared together, as he was always surrounded by friends. They were like newly-weds living with a tribe of in-laws.

Her karate instructor, Mike Stone, provided Priscilla with something Elvis rarely gave her: Attention.

As Elvis pondered alone amid the luxury and loneliness of the penthouse a part of him knew that he had lost everything he had ever wanted. That was the country boy, the kid who had been a truck driver, who wanted nothing more than a wife, a family and food on the table. But it had never been that way. Couldn't be. He was Elvis Presley.

Why could Priscilla not understand that? He was not just another man. Sure, there had been other women – lots of them – But the girls were not just an indulgence, they were also a duty. There were dreams to fulfil, fantasies to maintain, it was all part of being Elvis Presley, and being Elvis Presley was what had given her riches, jewellery, mansions, clothes.

He had given her everything. What more could money buy for a woman who had everything? He knew the answer: Nothing. She wanted nothing from him that money could buy – only his time – but did she not realize that his time *was* money.

·The arguments swirled around in his brain. He was angry with himself for losing the woman he loved. He was angry with Priscilla. He was angry with Mike Stone. He was angry with himself. He was the man who had everything, and suddenly it meant nothing. . .

It is said that Elvis demanded the life of Mike Stone, like a godfather, commanding his men to "Bring Me the Head of Alfredo Garcia." It is true – but only in the sense that it was an expression of the swelling anger inside. That he could have had Stone killed is beyond doubt. Among the Memphis Mafia there were certainly men who would die for him – perhaps there were one or two who would *kill* for him.

Had he looked outside his own men then he would not have found it difficult to hire a killer. Surely the proof that Elvis was reacting in the way any other cheated husband would have reacted – with ranting, empty threats – is still available today. In the shape of Mike Stone.

Another myth is that Elvis's physical decline dates from this time, but perhaps there had always been a question mark about his health. As far back as 1956 he had written in a letter to fan club members, "I'm six feet tall and I weigh 195 pounds and I've gained about 20 pounds in the last year. . . I can't understand that because my appetite isn't as good as it used to be. . . I can't seem to relax ever and I have a terrible time falling asleep at night. At the most I usually get two or three hours of broken sleep."

Throughout his life, even as a child, Elvis had suffered from insomnia. During his days in Hollywood he had taken sleeping pills to get a good night's rest before filming. But as the films began to pall, he often replaced a sleeping pill with a diet pill. It had several advantages. . . it made him feel good, by controlling his weight it made him look good, and he could stay up all night at parties. When he returned to live performances his lifestyle became permanently and irrevocably nocturnal. . . sleeping all day, performing and partying all night.

His split with Priscilla and subsequent divorce did not cause the deterioration of his health. But it did contribute to the depressions which led to his eating bouts. In turn, his eating bouts caused him to put on weight, which depressed him. These weight problems and crash diets increased his health problems and his reliance on pills.

Throughout the aching, empty days of spring, through the summer when the split was first made public, Elvis was comforted by one thought. One thing, one thing only, had remained faithful, loyal, constant in all these years. . . the devotion of his fans. From this point on Elvis dedicated himself to touring with an almost

THE ELVIS DIARY

9 March 1975
After almost six months of seclusion, Elvis spends three days in RCA Studios, Hollywood where he records several tracks, including I Can Help. *He then flies to Las Vegas for a fortnight in concert.*

3 May 1975
Elvis embarks on a gruelling two-week tour of the south.

31 December 1975
Elvis sees in the year performing for an audience of 80,000 at the Silver Dome in Pontiac, Michigan. His takings are $816,000 for the performance – the highest amount for a single night received by a single artist.

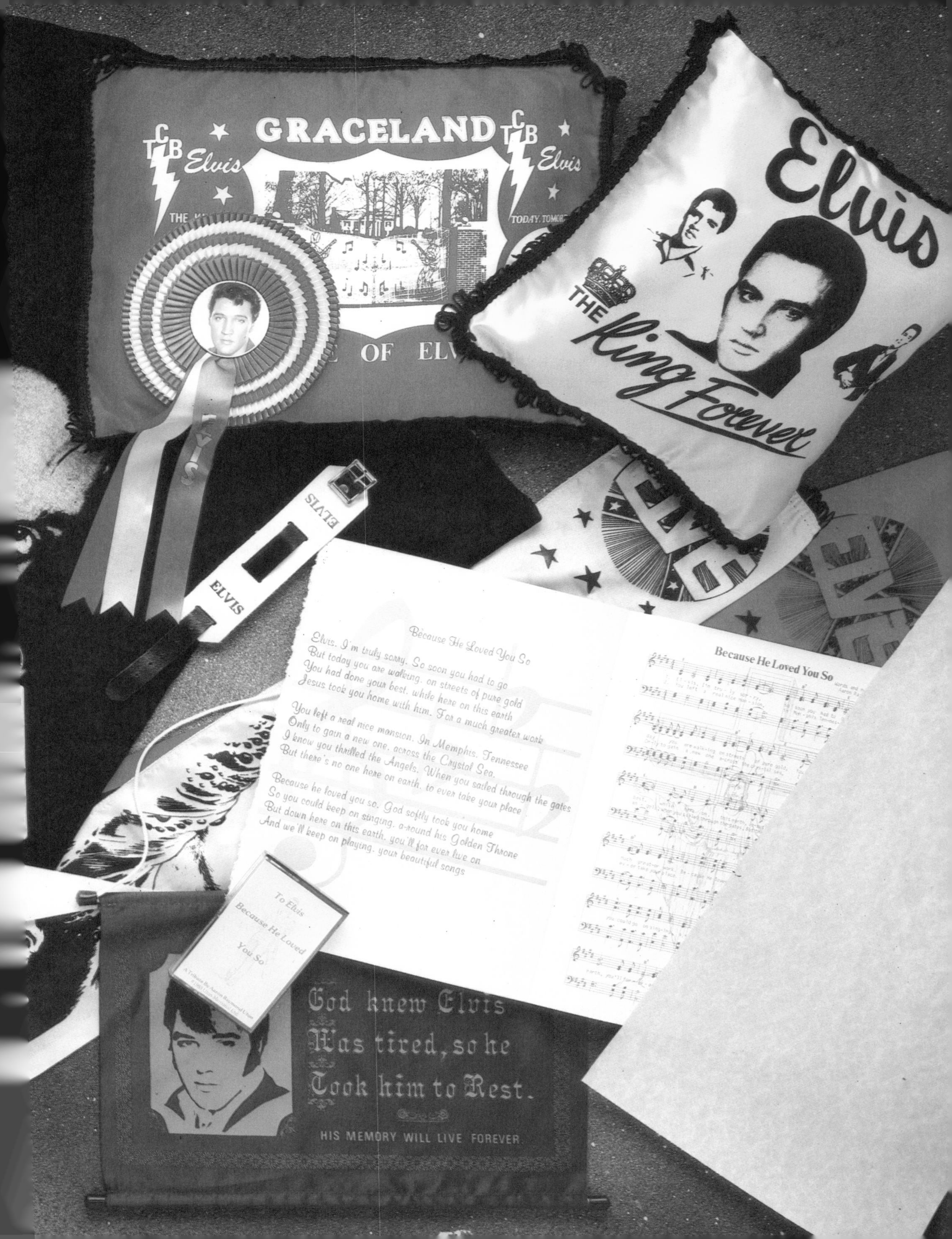

GRACELAND

TCB Elvis   TCB Elvis

THE ... OF ELVIS

TODAY, TOMOR...

Elvis

THE King Forever

ELVIS

Because He Loved You So

Elvis, I'm truly sorry. So soon you had to go
But today you are walking, on streets of pure gold
You had done your best, while here on this earth
Jesus took you home with him, for a much greater work

You left a real nice mansion, in Memphis, Tennessee
Only to gain a new one, across the Crystal Sea.
I know you thrilled the Angels, when you sailed through the gates
But there's no one here on earth, to ever take your place

Because he loved you so, God softly took you home
So you could keep on singing, a-round his Golden Throne
But down here on this earth, you'll for ever live on
And we'll keep on playing, your beautiful songs

Because He Loved You So

To Elvis
Because He Loved
You So

A Tribute ...

God knew Elvis
Was tired, so he
Took him to Rest.

HIS MEMORY WILL LIVE FOREVER.

THE ELVIS DIARY

February 1976
Elvis begins to use Graceland as a recording studio. The first album he records there is From Elvis Presley Boulevard.

23 August 1976
Elvis's autumn season at the Las Vegas Hilton is cancelled after three nights due to ill-health.

The King.

Messianic zeal, an evangelical fervour, a man whose mission was to bring himself and his music to his fans.

He gave orders for bigger shows, better shows, more tours, longer tours. With his appearances at Las Vegas, Elvis's itinerary began to read like an airline schedule. Recording sessions did not interest him – or inspire him. He wanted – seemed to need – the acclaim of his fans. It was as if he lived only for the charge he received from the lightning bolt that bounced between him and his fans. Off-stage he was often depressed, sinking into deep, lonely moods. He slept for as long as he could, waking only to prepare for the night's show.

On 19 October 1973 at the Santa Monica Superior Court, Elvis and Priscilla, in the words of his hit of the time went their "Separate Ways". They posed for photographs, arm in arm. They smiled and seemed friends. Indeed, Elvis and Priscilla did remain friends, but while Priscilla set off to build a new life, Elvis's life seemed to fall apart.

Just six days after the divorce Elvis was admitted to the Baptist Memorial Hospital in Memphis. It was the first of many hospital stays. The bulletins said that Elvis had been admitted to rest. They told the truth, but not the whole truth. The truth was that Elvis's body was wearing out. He was a sick man with a list of complaints that read like a medical dictionary. . . twisted colon, hypoglycaemia, breathing difficulties, an enlarged heart, glaucoma and blood clots in his legs.

While Elvis undoubtedly misused the drugs available to him there can be little doubt that he desperately needed a regular intake of what he always called his "medication" to keep the pain from his several ailments under control.

If, in 1973, Elvis had rested, stayed in hospital until he was truly fit, perhaps the doctors would have prolonged his life. But to Elvis. . . his fans, his tours, his shows were his life. A familiar pattern emerged: Elvis would drive himself into the ground on tour and then be forced to spend a period in hospital. In Memphis his fans always knew long before the media that Elvis had been admitted to his suite on the fifth floor of the Baptist Memorial Hospital – they could tell when the nurses started plastering the windows with aluminium foil so that Elvis could continue his nocturnal lifestyle.

By this point Elvis's crash diets were no longer able to control his weight – and he seemed unable to control his yearning for junk food like cheeseburgers, pizzas, cream cakes and crispy bacon. But to his fans middle-aged spread and midriff bulge didn't seem to matter. He was still one great-looking guy, still one helluva mover and still had the greatest voice. And he still filled every concert. Perhaps if his fans had been more critical, had stayed away, if the acclaim had died away, he might have been forced to take a long, hard look at himself, might have pulled himself around.

His fans, his friends and his family. . . they all pleaded with him to rest. But like a man possessed, he insisted on his punishing schedule: in 1974 he was on the road for six months with only short rests in between each tour – he did a total of 70 shows, not including his Vegas dates; in 1975, again not counting Las Vegas, he was touring for four months, doing a total of nearly sixty shows; in 1976 – his peak year – he was performing somewhere every month for ten months of the year. In 1977, the year he died, he had already done 55 shows in five months and was due to leave for another tour the day after he died.

His attitude was summed up by what he told an ecstatic Las Vegas audience in 1976. He would do more shows than ever before – "and hit every city".

In 1977, Elvis seemed to set out to do just that. On 8 January he celebrated his forty-second birthday at Graceland. He was not in the best of health, but he was in better spirits. The scars caused by his divorce were at last beginning to heal, and he even talked of marriage to his latest girlfriend, a 20-year-old Tennessee beauty called Ginger Alden. He would spend his time playing racquetball, watching TV or videos, reading, resting. . . and eating. In March, on a whim, he had the Guys pack his private jet, the *Lisa Marie,* and they all headed for Hawaii for a pre-tour holiday.

Elvis returned looking better than he had for months. For once there was colour in his cheeks. He had lost some weight and some

THE ELVIS DIARY

12 February 1977
Elvis begins a short tour of southern cities he has not visited previously. His overweight is very noticeable and is causing a great deal of concern.

March 1977
Elvis takes his last vacation in Hawaii.

March 1977
Elvis falls ill again and is readmitted to the Baptist Hospital.

The Last Vacation in Hawaii.

THE ELVIS DIARY

29 May 1977
Elvis walks off stage in mid-performance at the Baltimore Civic Centre, looking ill and exhausted. Although he returns to complete the show after a short break, his ailing appearance does not go unnoticed.

2 June 1977
After two more concerts in Georgia and Alabama Elvis returns to Memphis for a rest.

19 June 1977
CBS Television start filming Elvis on tour for their Special, Elvis In Concert.

26 June 1977
Elvis plays what is to be his last concert at Indianapolis.

1 August 1977
This date sees the publication of Elvis: What Happened—a book written by three of Elvis's former employees which claims that Elvis was guilty of drug abuse—a statement which deeply shocks Elvis.

3 August 1977
Elvis takes his daughter Lisa Marie out for the day in Memphis—the last time he is seen with Lisa Marie in public.

of the puffiness around the eyes, but on 31 March, before he was due to appear at Baton Rouge, Louisiana, Elvis was taken ill. The doctors diagnosed fatigue and intestinal flu. He was flown back to Memphis and his suite in the Baptist Memorial Hospital, where he stayed for just a few days before going home to Graceland.

In April, just two weeks later, Elvis – against all advice – went back on the road on a 12-city tour. He was touring again in May and again in June – when two dates at Omaha, Nebraska on 19 June and Rapid City, South Dakota, on 21 June were used as the basis for a CBS Special.

On 26 June at Indianapolis, Indiana, Elvis gave what was to be his final performance. The fans went wild after a brilliant show. Elvis was looking good as he usually did at the end of a rigorous tour. He raised his hand and with a wave left the stage. A few moments later, a familiar voice spoke those few familiar words that always signalled that the show was finally over. The voice said, "Ladies and Gentlemen. . . Elvis has left the building." For Elvis the show also was finally about to end.

He returned to Graceland where he began planning his next tour, due to begin at Portland, Maine, on 17 August. As always when he was resting he began to eat. As usual his weight ballooned again and he became depressed, but this time his moods were darker than usual.

At that time three bodyguards, including Red West, whom he had known since his high school days, had left his service and were writing a book about their experiences with Elvis. The book, *Elvis – What Happened,* was published at the beginning of August with massive publicity, and purported to show Elvis as a drug-crazed, homicidal maniac. Elvis was deeply hurt. Not so much by the allegations but by the thought that three men he had loved and cared for could have betrayed him.

He threw himself into the last-minute planning of his August tour – even the younger members of his entourage found the schedule gruelling. It was a crippling, crushing, punishing programme demanded by no-one but Elvis.

The people around him felt it was like trying to stop a runaway truck. . . without knowing how to apply the brakes, and they whispered their worries among themselves. It's as if he is trying to work himself to death. . .

BEWARE THE MIDDLE-CLASS MENACE! PAGE THREE

Heart attack after a hard game of squash

ELVIS, KING OF ROCK, DIES AT 42

ELVIS PRESLEY, the rock star whose pelvic wiggle and p r i m e v a l scream launched contemporary pop music, died last night, apparently of a heart attack. He was 42.

The king of rock 'n' roll was grossly overweight, experiencing eye trouble and deeply depressed at rapidly advancing middle age.

But it was a particularly strenuous game of racket ball— American squash — at Presley's Memphis mansion that finally led to his death.

Elvis, exhausted and dripping with sweat, told friends he could go on no longer.

He said he was going to his bedroom to lie down because suddenly he felt very tired.

His friends teased him and carried on playing. When he did not appear an hour later they went to his bedroom and knocked on the door. There was no reply.

They broke into the room and found Presley slumped on the bathroom floor. He was dead.

Too old to Rock: Page 16

He was taken by ambulance — with his doctor pleading 'Breathe, Presley, breathe' — to the Baptist Hospital in Memphis. Last night, as hundreds of m o u r n i n g fans besieged the hospital, doctors said they would not be able to confirm the heart attack until a post mortem had been carried out.

There were incredible scenes across America as radio and TV stations broke the news. Switchboards were jammed as fans demanded confirmation.

For weeks rumours have circulated in showbiz circles that Presley was seriously ill and was being kept alive only by drugs.

Only this week sections of a new book on Presley were published in America. One of the three authors — all former Elvis bodyguards — said: He believed the singer

From RODERICK GILCHRIST in New York

was committing 'slow suicide' with his drug taking.

The writer, Dave Habler, said: 'It is hard for me to understand how he can deliberately set out to destroy himself. It seems he is bent on death.'

Two weeks ago Elvis, once slim-hipped and lean limbed, ballooned up to nearly 17 stone, six stone heavier than his once trim 11 stone frame, but despite urgings from his doctor he ate huge meals and was constantly having snacks.

Presley, the idol in the gold lamé suit with the sullen smoulder, serpentine moves, sideburns and greased black hair, sold more records than the Beatles.

The quietly-spoken truck driver rose to fame in 1956 by breaking dramatically away from the squeaky clean image of the teen idols of the day. He gave adolescents all over the world a sensual mixture of Southern country and rhythm and blues.

He still appeared regularly in the pop charts even though he was to many an overweight joke figure who no longer deserved his crown.

Initially an anti-establishment figure condemned for his highly-charged sexual stage act — they called him Elvis the Pelvis— Presley's biggest hits are still performed today by rock bands.

Presley's first hit was the slow-

Turn to Page 3, Col. 1

Elvis Presley . . . he was depressed over middle age.

Tories blame the Red Fascists

Daily Mail Reporter

LEADING Tory Front Bencher Michael Heseltine last night attacked the Socialist Workers Party as the extremists responsible for this week's political street violence.

The party were, he said, reincarnation of Hitler Brownshirt's 'under the disguise of Karl Marx'.

As Mr Heseltine launched his savage attack, Scotland Yard Commissioner Mr David McNee revealed that the police were considering bringing charges against the party leaders for incitement to riot.

And as the political temperature rose throughout the day the Government nervously announced that it may bring in new legislation to amend the old Public Order Act brought in to stop the Mosleyite riots in 1936.

Brave

But this will clearly not be enough for the Tories.

Speaking in Ladywood, Birmingham, 24 hours after the riots and two days before the constituency goes to the poll, Mr Heseltine said it was the extreme Left which had lit the fuse of violence.

'The failure of the Government to support our forces of law and order is an appalling comment on them,' he said.

'The truth is that the Labour Party itself is riddled by Left-Wing extremists that in any conflict between the extreme Left and the forces of law and order it is paralysed and unable to support those brave men and women who are upholding not only law, but also the basic liberties of our citizens.'

'The Left is on the march armed with a new weapon, street violence, and the Government lacks the will and in some cases the inclination, to back the thin blue line of the forces of law who stand between the majority and t h e anti-democratic minority of political hooligans.'

Pressure

'In attacking the police in this way, the Left have made a grave error. The British police are the finest in the world.

'Their courage and restraint under extreme pressure and actual physical assault is unequalled.

'The Conservative Party backs the police in its efforts to maintain rule of law at Grunwick, at Lewisham and now at Birmingham 100 per cent.'

As the Government is under heavy fire for failing

Turn to Page 2, Col.

Chapter Eleven

THE
KING
IS
DEAD

"There's no way to measure his impact on society or the void that he leaves. He will always be the King of Rock'n'Roll." *Pat Boone*

On a drilling rig far out in the North Sea, an oil worker gazed unseeingly into the blackness, dreaming of home. Another man approached him and quietly murmured a few words. The first man turned, his eyes bright with fury. He kept his cool but his voice was ice-cold: "If you ever say that to me again – even as a joke – I'll tear you apart."

The other man was shaken, as shocked by his news as the reaction it had evoked. "It's true," he said. "I wouldn't joke. . . not about something like this."

Within a few minutes the first man had broken down. He was in hysterics. Uncontrollable. Inconsolable. Within an hour a helicopter had been flown from the mainland to the oil rig especially to take him off. His behaviour was considered a danger to the safety of the rig.

In St Louis, a young woman heard the news. She had been saving hard, looking forward to the day she would marry her sweetheart. Saving for the future. Suddenly the future didn't seem to matter. She leapt into her car, drove to the bank, withdrew every cent she had, and caught the next available plane to Memphis.

Outside the gates of a mansion in Memphis, a vast crowd began to gather, expecting an announcement to say that the rumours they'd heard were nothing more than a hoax.

As the news came through on radio stations all over the world, people stopped what they were doing, the moment frozen for ever in memory.

Radio and television programmes were interrupted with the news. Then programmes were abandoned altogether and the air time given over completely to music, his music. Not the slow, sombre, mournful music of death, but rock 'n' roll, the music of life. And as the world waited still to be told it just was not true, that the impossible, the unthinkable, the unbearable had not really happened, the newspapers, in cold black and white, indelible and undeniable, hit the streets in a thousand cities.

Elvis est mort. . . Elvis está muerto. . . Elvis ist tot. . . Elvis è morto. . Elvis is dood. . .Elvis ni mfu. . .

ELVIS IS DEAD.

THE ELVIS DIARY
16 August 1977
Ginger Alden finds Elvis slumped on the floor of his bathroom at Graceland. Although he is rushed to Baptist Memorial Hospital, he was already dead. The tragic announcement of his death is made to the world at 3.30 p.m.

It is a moment scarred in a million memories, the moment they learned that Elvis Presley was dead. Only the death of assassinated American President John F. Kennedy is as brutally branded upon the public consciousness.

16 August 1977. . . the Greatest Entertainer in the World, Elvis Presley was dead and something of the world had died with him.

The 24 hours that were to be the last Elvis would spend on this earth began just like any of the other days Elvis spent at Graceland while he rested in between his ever-increasing tour schedule. He awoke mid-afternoon and called for his breakfast – just coffee – he was on one of his strength-sapping, battering crash diets in preparation for the tour due to begin on 17 August.

Outside, the sun streamed down remorselessly, baking the pavements and half-cooking the people. The heat was heavy and oppressive. But inside his bedroom at Graceland Elvis was cool. He kept the room temperature there several degrees lower than the rest of the house. "Cold enough to hang meat," someone had once remarked.

Elvis called down for some more coffee – and some company. Lisa Marie joined him. She was on her longest-ever stay with her father and was due to go home to her mother the day Elvis left on tour . . . Some of the Guys drifted in . . . Billy Smith, his cousin, and Charlie Hodge, his friend, and the jester at the court of the King. Joe Esposito, the road manager, popped in and out constantly, hassled and harassed with last-minute details of the tour, seeking Elvis's OK on any changes.

Elvis spent the rest of the day with Charlie, Billy and Ginger Alden, his latest girlfriend, watching snatches of television and discussing with Charlie the latest book he was reading, called *The Shroud*. He was nervy, due to the prospect of the tour, and also the prospect of a visit that night to a dentist to have a crown fixed on a back tooth. But he had other problems too. Despite his crash diet he was overweight. With the tour about to start he knew he did not look his best, and that worried him. Elvis never liked to give his fans anything less than his absolute best. Added to this he was about to face his fans for the first time since the publication of the book by his former bodyguards Red and Sonny West and Dave Hebler, which contained such hurtful and potentially damaging allegations about his lifestyle.

Las Vegas in 1976.

He was worried about how the fans would react to him. He needn't have worried – the fanatical loyalty and undying devotion that has remained in all the years since his death, would have pulled him through those first few anxious days.

The atmosphere between Elvis and Ginger Alden was strained. Ginger had spent six weeks at Graceland with Elvis. She said she wanted a break, some time by herself. She didn't want to go on tour. Elvis couldn't understand this – he loved her and wanted her with him all the time. If she loved him she would want to be with him, he argued, but Ginger would not budge. Billy and Charlie, sensing the atmosphere, tried to jolly Elvis out of his mood, talking about *The Shroud* and topics that came up on one of the three televisions he watched simultaneously.

At 10.30 p.m., Elvis, Ginger, Billy and Charlie piled into the Black Stutz to visit his dentist, Dr Lester Hoffman. Elvis had two teeth fixed and then left for home. At about 1.30 a.m., 16 August 1977, the Black Stutz slowed as it reached the gates of Graceland. As usual, when Elvis was at home, there was a group of fans on a midnight vigil. Elvis looked out and smiled. The fans may have made him a virtual prisoner in his own home, but their devotion was something he could not live without.

One of the fans spotted him and pressed the button of his camera. The flash exploded and, like so many millions of times over the years, the face of Elvis Presley was captured on film.

Except. . . this was to be the last picture ever taken of Elvis Presley during his life-time.

For a couple of hours, Elvis called Billy and invited him to play racquetball in the court he had had built at the back of the mansion. He was sweating after the game and Billy washed and dried his hair. Then Billy went home to snatch a few hours sleep.

At 9 a.m. Elvis, in his blue silk pyjamas, picked up his copy of *The Shroud* and told Ginger he was going to the lounge area of his bathroom to read. Ginger closed her eyes and in seconds was asleep. Five hours later she awoke from a dream. . . to discover a nightmare.

Ginger called Elvis's name as she realized he was not in bed. She walked to the bathroom door, calling softly, thinking he might have fallen asleep in the black lounger chair. She pushed at the door but it would move only a few inches. She gazed down and through the crack she saw that Elvis had slumped forward out of the chair and was lying on his face.

She called downstairs for help. Within moments, Joe Esposito and Al Strada were in the bedroom, entering through a second door. Joe and Al tried to give Elvis the kiss of life as they heard the howl of the ambulance siren, racing up the highway.

Vernon Presley, frail and weak and just recovering from a heart attack, came into the bathroom. Next came the ambulancemen followed by Dr George Nichopoulos, Elvis's private physician. All the way to the Baptist Memorial Hospital, for seven long miles, the medics continued to work on Elvis and Dr Nick could be heard pleading, "Breathe, Presley, breathe." At the Baptist Memorial, an expert team of cardiac specialists was already on standby, and took over the attempts to revive him.

The emergency work continued for an hour in a resuscitation unit on the ground floor. Elvis's closest friends waited in an adjoining room, willing him to breathe while barely able to draw breath themselves. Then the adjoining door opened, Dr Nick, head bowed, walking so slowly he barely moved, came through the door.

The room fell totally quiet, fearful. Even the sound of weeping subsided into silence. Dr Nick raised his eyes and stared into the

THE ELVIS DIARY

18 August 1977
Crowds estimated at over 100,000 pack into Memphis for the funeral, although only family and close friends are present at the ceremony. Elvis is buried in Forest Hill Cemetery, next to his mother.

2 October 1977
Because of fears that Elvis's body will be stolen by fans, it (together with his mother's remains) is removed and buried in the Meditation Gardens at Graceland.

6 December 1977
The road running between Tupelo and Memphis is renamed "The Elvis Aaron Presley Memorial Highway".

Hearse Carrying the Body of Elvis Presley Heads for His Memphis Home

Thousands of Fans Gather For Last Glimpse of Elvis

NEW YORK, WEDNESDAY, AUGUST 17, 1977

Thousands Mourn

KING ELVIS

Elvis Pr

Elvis: Idol Of Millions

Army changed Elvis Presley, ...ed him. But there were still ...od years, more movies, more records, more millions, before loneliness and a broken marriage signaled the beginning of the end. He became a virtual recluse, trapped by his fans and his fame, venturing out only to work. Yet he worked, and was idolized, to the end. See Lonely in a Crowd, the last in a series by Alton Slagle, on page 29.

Thousands mourn Elvis

MEMPHIS, Tenn. (AP)—Only a few, a token few among the adoring millions, viewed the body of Elvis Presley as it lay in his mansion Wednesday in a seamless copper coffin. The singer's privacy was as guarded in death as it was in life.

Thousands of Presley fans pushed and shoved for one last glimpse of their idol, ...ing in the steel-lined coffin.

... of the entertainer's fans had driv...away as Texas for a 10-sec... ...nger's body, dressed ...lue shirt and

precedented and will probably never be equalled."

Others noted the passing of the King of Rock 'n' Roll in record stores across the country. Store owners reported heavy sales of Presley records, with most of their customers picking up several of the discs that made him a household name.

A shopkeeper in Charleston, W.Va., reported that two women scuffled briefly over his last copy of "Moody Blue." Presley's latest album.

As fans around the world mourned Presley, others came to Graceland mansion, his elegant Memphis home and refuge. ...the crowd began to gather before dawn ...ued to grow into the thousands ...on. ...resley's mansion

were closed to the public at 7:3 EDT police estimated there we some 15,000 people gathered outsi

The crowd, reluctantly at first dispersing when a police of nounced over an electronic r that no more people would be the mansion.

The Presley family, wh planned to permit public body from 4-6 p.m. (E mansion gates to rema minutes because of th

It was estimated t Presley fans passed their last respects

After the publi coffin was clos in a crypt nea

'This is Lisa. Daddy is dead.'

NASHVILLE, Tenn. (AP) — "This is Lisa. My daddy is dead."

The quivering voice on the phone belonged to 9-year-old Lisa Marie Presley, who was breaking the tragic news of her famous father's death to his former sweetheart, Linda Thompson.

"No, baby, he's not dead," the 28-year-old ex-beauty queen said she assured Elvis Presley's only child, not knowing that the rock 'n' roll singer had died about

Elvis' chief bodyguard for the past years.

"He's not really dead, is he?" Li cried.

"Yes, he is," answered Thompson, former Shelby County Sheriff's Patr lieutenant. "You'd better come t Memphis."

Lisa's mother, Priscilla Presley, also was in Los Angeles and both rushed to Memphis.

Linda, who recently was in Nashville filming a role in the Hee Haw television series, had met Elvis in 1971 at a Memphis movie house he had rented for a group of friends to join him in seeing a movie.

Almost immediately began dat...

DAILY NEWS

New York, Thursday, August 18, 1977

housands Pay Tribute at Elvis' Bier

Adoring Fans Wait in Line
Hoping for One Last Look

Memphis, Tenn. (UPI) — The body of Elvis Presley was borne behind the iron gates of Graceland mansion yesterday— gates finally opened to the rock singer's adoring fans.

The city of Memphis lowered its flags to half staff Carter praised Presley as a symbol of the coun- liousness and good humor."

Presley, 42, collapsed and di— of a bathroom near his be— room mansion. The a severely irregular

Thousands waite who mesmerized his yo they waited, they entwi The white hearse tl

Elvis Presley: The King Is Dead

ELVIS PRESLEY'S death at age 42 has left a significant segment of the nation in shock, a fact which again confirms the impact the man had on the American scene.

He was more than a popular enter- ainer with the ability to capture the ive light of — ress for more than — He w— within the — especially

Some critics who wrote kindly Elvis believe he portrayed the i a working class rebel.

Of course he enjoyed his sl good luck that is bestowe successful people, the m slice coming perhaps whe up with his promoter. "C as Parker. "Don't expla it," was the Colonel's Elvis even was given his musical ability, o feelings he was able

The Presley pow roll, a new

THE MIAMI HERALD   Thursday

Thousands See Elvis and an Era Interred

Toni Catron of Stone Mountain, Ga., cries at gate of Presley mansion. *Associated Press photo*

Elvis: A Soiled American Dream

Memphis—Through the night, some of them waited in the Hickory Log Restaurant (break- fast 24 hours a day) right across Elvis Presley Blvd. from the estate called Graceland. They sipped cof- fee and ate doughnuts and talked about death, and then in the day- time, they moved across the street, lining up against the pink stone wall. Others listened to radios in parked cars, or stayed at home and played all the old records. Some piled into pickup trucks, and drove up from Mississippi, drinking beer along the way, going to say goodbye to the boy from Tupelo.

"He was the first singer I ever really recognized," said Grace Corri- gan, from Memphis. "The first name that was different from others. T rest of them were just m—

PETE HAMILL

was Elvis, and I was 6 years old and know it was him."

Grace Corrigan is 26, and she was jammed behind the police barricades near the gates of the estate. The people were 12 deep up there, squashed against each other in the wet heat. And a lot of them peered over the wall — cool trimmed lawn a— de trees and — mns of the — h a d lived. — ny envy in

them. And not, to be truthful, much grace.

"It's sad a man that young going that fast," said Casrolyn Woods, a black woman from Memphis. "A man who had everything: ood looks, lots of money, plenty of cars, and I guess all the girls he wanted. It's a shame But you know, he had a good lif while it lasted."

Heat Gets to Them

Now they were all standing in brutal Southern heat, choking in fumes of the two-mile-long lir cars that was cruising past being shoved by the cops, and views by strangers. More thar them collapsed with heat pro: Or simple excitement. And a had to do with saying goo dead rock 'n' roll singer nar

(Continued on page 19,

Presley Family Plot at Forest Hills in Memphis
... Elvis will be buried there near his mother
— Associated Press

Neighborhood Fans
Survived on Glimpses
Of Star and Handou

Shake,

lutio— the

really serious part seemed to turn to It brought him we

It was summ stopped by the of Co. in Memphis record. He ha father Vernon had no forma never did hav music.

That rec he took it F A year lat cut anoth company. released tion. But Kentucky." wa—

Disc jockeys began stic— version of the old bluegrass classic

South. It v gospel choi ches on Su hillbilly ba little groups in smoky tav ton land on Sa blues from the Mississippi delta. It was Hank Williams and Little
Lightnin' Hopkins.

'vis nd el— ne would uch, run down cramble up to the plat- would stand looking at the noir and try to sing with them. He was too little to know the words, but he could carry the tune."

The Presleys were a popular singing trio — his twin brother Jesse Garon had died at birth — at the camp meet- ings and revivals and church conven- — popular in the South in those faces of Charlie and Billy, and as he caught the look of childlike faith in their eyes and sensed the hope in their hearts, his body trembled and the words seemed to be shaken from his soul.

"Oh my God," he sobbed. "He's gone."

Larry Geller had wanted to say No. Hated saying Yes. But how could he refuse? How could he refuse the request of a man who had just lost his only son? How could he refuse one last favour to a friend? A friend who had refused him nothing? Vernon Presley had called him. Just one more time, Larry, just once, would you cut Elvis's hair? You know he would want to look his best. You can do it, Larry. Only you. You always did it better. Please.

But could he do it? He had cut Elvis's hair so many times before. This time it was different. This time would be the last time. Elvis is dead, he said to himself, and still he could not believe it.

The black Cadillac edged its way inch by inch through the gates of Graceland, police and troopers clearing a path through the crush of grieving people who had laid siege to the mansion in the few short hours since the death of Elvis Presley was announced.

A few of the fans recognized Larry's companion, Charlie Hodge, who had shared so many years with Elvis, shared so many hours with him by his side on stage. Larry glanced at Charlie. His eyes were empty and he gazed vacantly ahead. Larry knew that if Charlie had not agreed to come with him, he could never have made it on his own.

The car at last nudged its path through the fringes of the crowd and picked up speed as it made its way along Elvis Presley Boulevard to the Memphis Funeral Home where Elvis's body had been sent to be embalmed.

A funeral director, with exaggerated ceremony, closed the doors of the Chapel of Rest behind Larry and Charlie. Larry heard the soft, almost inaudible, slow, sombre music and, across the room, saw Elvis lying bathed in a pale glowing light. "Elvis," he gushed, feeling the surge of pleasure he always felt when he entered the presence of The Boss. "Elvis," he said again, still with the same sound of surprise and joy in his voice. He expected Elvis to get up, smile, crack a joke. For a third time he said, "Elvis." But this time it was an empty, lonely sound, hopeless, joyless, lifeless. Larry Geller knew then that Elvis Presley was really dead.

ELVIS

Death of Elvis strike
mournful chord in E

Waterbury Republican, Thursday, August 18, 1977—11

Record stores sell out
of Presley's recordings

By MARC CHARNEY
Associated Press Writer

From Portland, Ore. to Portland, Maine, fans, collectors and speculators reacted to Elvis Presley's death by rushing out to record stores and snapping up his albums.

Record stores across the country reported a run on Presley recordings on Tuesday and Wednesday that left their stocks sold out or sharply depleted by the time 24 hours had passed.

"One woman, probably in her early 20s, bought six eight-tracks of Elvis," said Lynne Franklin, whose husband owns Al Franklin Musical World in the Hartford, Conn., Civic Center. "Then she asked the salesman what she played them on. When told, she went to the front of the store and bought an eight-track player."

"We're sold out — LPs, eight-tracks and cassettes," said Mrs. Franklin. "It's mostly middle-aged people who want the Elvis recordings. It's absolutely amazing."

It was so amazing that Evelyn Dalrymple in Omaha, Neb., Charles Young in Huntington, W.Va., Ruth Baker in Portland, Maine, Ben Asner in Kansas City, and Oscar Glickman in Big Spring, Texas — all of whom run record stores — came up with the same reaction:

"I've never seen anything like it."

Descriptions of the average purchaser varied — weeping fans in Birmingham,

Ala.; unemotional collectors in Portland, Ore.; an elderly woman in Springfield, Mass., who had never owned an Elvis record but liked the songs he sang.

In Fort Lauderdale, Fla., a record store manager said a man wrote a check for $250 that wouldn't clear. He managed to scrape up the cash.

In Charleston, W.Va., two women scuffled briefly at the National Record Mart as both tried to buy the store's last copy of "Moody Blue," Presley's most recent album. A clerk said one woman had put down the album while looking at other Presley records. The second woman came along and grabbed it.

A spokesman in Indianapolis for RCA Records, for which Presley had recorded since 1956, said the plant there had sold 250,000 copies of "Moody Blue" alone on Wednesday.

"We're not trying to commercialize this," another spokesman at RCA said. "We're just trying to meet the demand."

RCA's Indianapolis plant, which had been pressing "Moody Blue" to meet demand of about 100,000 copies a week, went on a 24-hour, seven-days-a-week schedule, the spokesman said.

RCA says that in 1975, Presley's lifetime sales surpassed 500 million records. A record industry source said the current boom might add another 100 million.

"We started running out right away Tuesday afternoon," said Jim Cowan, an

employe at Everybody's Record Store in Portland, Ore. "Now we're down to three albums. We tried to order more last night, but RCA's Northwest distributor in Seattle was out within an hour."

"For the most part they appea collectors, not really th Cowan. "They up."

A harried Shop in Big S izes in oldies, other in the 42 business.

"A lot of time have people con buy some of the ol a different deal. M 'em are women — not all younger, a They're not happy. when they come in, records."

"Nobody is buying j buying all they can get. of deal, I tell you."

It was the same at the N Mart in Cincinnati, whe Elaine McKulka said the Elvis records and tapes sol hours.

"We put an album on to play bought it right off the phonogr said.

Continued on Page D18, Col. 1

ELVIS PRESLEY DIES; ROCK SINGER WAS 42

He Is Found Unconscious at Home — Acclaim Followed Scorn

BY MOLLY IVINS

Elvis Presley, the first and greatest American rock-and-roll star, has died at the age of 42. Mr. Presley, whose throaty baritone and blatant sexuality redefined popular music, was found unconscious in the bedroom of his home, called Graceland, in Memphis yesterday at 2:30 P.M. He was taken to Baptist Hospital, where doctors aempted to revive him, and was pronounced dead of respiratory failure at 3:50 P.M.

Mr. Presley was once the object of such adulation that teen-age girls screamed and fainted at the sight of him. He was also denounced for what was considered sexually suggestive conduct on stage. Preachers inveighed against him in sermons and parents forbade their children to watch him on television. In his first television appearance on the Ed Sullivan show, his act, which might be thought of as tame by today's standards, was considered by the broadcasters to be so scandalous that the cameras showed him only from the waist up, lest his wiggling hips show.

Mr. Presley's early hit songs are an indelible part of the memories of anyone who grew up in the 50's. "Hound Dog," "Heartbreak Hotel," and "Blue Suede Shoes" were teen-age anthems. Like

Presley Gave Rock Its Style

He Didn't Invent Form, But Did Bestow Image

BY JOHN ROCKWELL

For most people, Elvis Presley was rock-and-roll. And they were right. Bill Haley may have made the first massive rock hit, and people such as Chuck Berry and Little Richard may have had an equally important creati impact on this raucous n American art form. Bu

An Appraisal

was Elvis who defined style and gave it an im image. The songs were tough and in a time, 20 years ago, when A popular music was still based Pan Alley tune-smithing. And was of a working-class r sex into the nation's conscie before the "sexual revolut ominous, greasy, swirlin tions, Elvis was a perfo leather jacket and his ag ents abhorred, young w young men instantly

Presley's national spring of 1956, afte RCA Victor, in th such hits as "H first), "Don't Be (a double-sided and "Love Me But before style in Sam in Memphis.

Cont

Slowly, methodically, instinctively, he started snipping away at Elvis's raven locks, preparing them as he had done so many times before. Except that this time he worked in silence. All the other times they had talked. Talked of many things – God and gods, religion and religions, philosophies, meanings. Mysteries. . . mankind, the universe, God, love, life. And death.

Larry would bring him books on mysticism and theology and they would talk for hours. Elvis called Larry "My Guru". But this time there was no conversation – just the silence and the snip, snip, snip of his scissors and the soft, sad sound of the requiem. At times Larry felt faint, his knees would buckle and his eyes would blur. Charlie, staring deeply into nothing, would notice the lapses and hold a steadying hand to his arm. Finally, Larry pulled the comb through Elvis's hair and began to tidy away. From his pocket he took a handkerchief and gently and tenderly brushed the cuttings into the square of silk.

As they rode back to Graceland one of them flicked the switch of the radio. The station was playing Elvis music non-stop, interrupted only by the latest bulletin of the gathering masses besieging the mansion and the thousands more who had booked every aeroplane and form of transport into Memphis.

The tributes were pouring in. The President of the United States, Jimmy Carter, said, "Elvis Presley's death deprives our country of a part of itself. He was one of a kind and irreplaceable. He was a symbol for the vitality, rebelliousness and the humour of this country for the whole world."

"There's no way to measure his impact on society or the void that he leaves. He will always be the King of Rock 'n' Roll."   *Pat Boone*

The world has lost its greatest ever entertainer, a pioneer, a symbol of change, youth, sex, style. An idol.

Larry leaned forward and flicked off the radio. He and Charlie had lost a friend.

The next day – 17 August 1977 – the body of Elvis Presley was taken home to Graceland. He was dressed in a white suit his father had given him for Christmas, a pale blue shirt and a yellow tie. As a gesture to the fans Vernon agreed that Elvis would "lie in state", to be viewed by the public from noon until 6.30 p.m.

Larry Geller walked to the copper-lined casket to put the last few finishing touches to Elvis's hair. Larry heard himself gasp. The pained, tormented expression that twisted Elvis's face the night before, had faded – instead there was a look, almost a glow, of contentment. Elvis was at peace.

For three and a half hours about 30,000 people filed through the gates, inching up the winding drive under the trees to the

will leaves bu...
...e estate to family

...(UPI) — Rock 'n'
Presley, who died
...rt failure at age 42,
...s enormous estate to
...ing to a will read in
...oday.

...e Joseph W. Evans
...ument introduced as
...will and testament and
...id it will be "the biggest
...e state of
...no inven
...mpany th
...o such an
... later.
...62-year-
...ted exec
...in Mar
...witnesse
...Hodge
...ng othe
...Presl
...and, w
...eek.

...LLOW
...s and
...prov
...st fun
...ar-old
...s gra
...erno

If Presle...
...are dead by the t...
...age of 25, she receives the e...
There was no provision in the...
page will for Miss Alden, who said Presley had planned to announce their engagement later this month, or for his
ex-wife, Priscill...aulieu, Lisa's
mother, who rur...hop in Los
Angeles.
"It is unlike...

for any future wife at this time," the
judge told UPI. "He would have rewrit-
ten his will if he had been married."
The judge said he also felt certain
child support going to Priscilla, his former wife, would stop since it would be
superseded by the child's inheritance.

THE WILL APPEARS To give Vernon
Presley iron-clad control over distribu-
tion of the wealth.
"There are no special bequests, like
...g an automobile to this one or a
...rs for that one. There are
...left up to Vernon
...dge Evans
...only
...ciary,
...major
...hare of
...ed for in
...'s mother
...h him.
...ill serve as
...rshal (inven-
...the judge said.
...he had a corpo-
...he executor will
...n of the court to
...for a period of six

...will probably be
...before the estate is

...finally...
In addition to the inventory Vernon
Presley makes of the assets, state and
federal tax departments will make
their own inventory to determine the
amount of inheritance taxes to be paid.

> *'The pitiful thing about
> it is that everyone is so
> dependent on Elvis, they
> know no other way of
> making a living. They're
> become accustomed to
> being guards and so on,
> and living a pretty com-
> fortable life. I don't
> know what they'll do
> now ...'*
>
> — Nancy Pease

ONE YEAR AFTER THE KING'S DEATH.

midnight GLOBE

VOL.25—NO. 32 (R) AUGUST 8, 1978 (F) 35c

8 PAGE SPECIAL SOUVENIR PULLOUT

THE REAL ELVIS

Elvis: The Memory Will Linger On

PETE HAMILL

Memphis, Tenn. — They left
Graceland mansion in 16 white
limousines, gleaming in the hot,
bright afternoon sun, and moved north
along Elvis Presley Blvd. This was the
last journey, and the copper, steel-lined
coffin carrying the king of rock 'n roll
lya in the dark of one of the cars, as
they passed through the city where he
had spent most of his life. They went
past gas stations and Dunkin' Donut
shops, past yards full of boats and
campers, and signs that said: "Goodbye
Elvis" and "You're Still The King" and
"We will always remember you."

They pulled over some bridges, and
up a hill, and then the crowds on the
right were larger and they were waving
handkerchiefs, and snapping pictures,
and some of them were crying. A car
full of Shriners in clown costumes went
by first, and a few people booed. The
Shriners waved and grinned in a ghast-

ly way, and then two more of them
came by wearing fezzes, driving dune
buggies. They were att4ending a convention here, but everyone else was
waiting for the 16 white limousines.
"I just came out to say goodbye,"
said Aggie Mulholland, a black woman
who lived intheghettoonthefarside
of the Forest Hill Cemetery. "He was a
good-hearted man. He was good to black
folk, too.

Beyond the wall, they could see the
long sloping lawns of the cemetery.

with flowers in little vases placed beside slabs. Cops from the city and the
county had been joined by cemetery
guards, and they were working hard
this time trying to keep the crowds
orderly. Early yesterday morning, two
ggirls had been killed in front of Presley's mansion while talking to a cop. A
hit-and-run driver smashed into them,
and was caught after a chase.
"We ain't foolin' around today," one
of the city cops said. "We ain't gonna
lose any more people."

Sense of Anticlimax

When the cars of the funeral pr-
ocession finally went by, there was a
sense of anticlimax. These people had
been hearing Presley songs almost con-
tinuously for two days now, and they
had read all the stories in the special

(Continued on page 28, col. 1)

17 years!

to aid home preservation

...Miss. (UPI) — The boyhood
...Elvis Presley, a small white
...ouse, will be preserved with
...of a memorial trust fund.
...elo Mayor Clyde Whittaker said a
...ission would be named to deter-
...ine the memorial funds would

The house, similar to many built
during the depression era, currently is
managed by the Tupelo Park and
Recreation Department. Presley
donated $10,000 to restore the house in
1956 and it is now surrounded by a 15-
acre park with a swimming pool and
other recreational facilities.

- **Ginger Alden speaks about the last days**
- **Experts claim Elvis didn't have to die**
- **Elvis' life in pictures... 1953—1977**

house where the casket was on view. A stream of people. A river of tears. Deep in the shuttered house, the people who knew him, lived with him, loved him, stayed away, locked inside their own private misery, counting their own personal loss.

The fans who came that day, stayed the night keeping up their vigil of grief. It cost two of them their lives – a maniac driver ploughed into a crowd of fans opposite the mansion, killing two teenage girls instantly and severely crippling another. Across from Graceland, the Hickory Log stayed open around the clock, supplying the Cokes, hamburgers, fries, beers – and toilet facilities.

If the fans outside didn't sleep that night, the family and friends in Graceland couldn't sleep. Daybreak brought the morning not one of them – inside or out – ever dreamed would dawn.

Shortly before two that afternoon, Dee Presley, Vernon's ex-wife – helped by her sons, Billy, Ricky and David – walked into the living-room. She gazed at Elvis with a lost, bewildered look on her face. She tried to comfort Vernon but he was beyond soft words. She spoke briefly to Priscilla Presley, looking beautiful, elegant and composed. She whispered to Dee, "I will not cry. I must not cry."

Priscilla looked at her nine-year-old daughter Lisa Marie, who had never left the foot of her father's coffin, so quiet, so shy, so vulnerable. So like her father. "For Lisa's sake – I cannot cry."

At two the 150 people who had meant the most to Elvis crowded into the music room for a short service. Vernon, Priscilla and Lisa sat in the front row, and scattered around the room were former girlfriends – Linda Thompson, Ginger Alden, Ann-Margret. Somewhere at the back stood Colonel Parker in shirtsleeves. He knew that was how Elvis would expect him to behave. Outrageous, irreverent. As the Colonel. Even at a funeral.

One of Elvis's favourite female singers sang *My Heavenly Father Watches Over Me* and James Blackwood sang the title song of Elvis's 1967 gospel LP *How Great Thou Art*. This was followed by a short address, given by a pastor of a nearby church, C. W. Bradley, a long-time friend of the Presleys. Then Jacky Kahane, the comic who always appeared on Elvis's shows, stood up to speak. It was Jacky who had always ended an Elvis concert with the legendary words, "Ladies and Gentlemen. . . Elvis has left the building." It was perhaps appropriate that it was Jacky who should now bring the great show that was Elvis's life to an end with the words, "Ladies and Gentlemen. . . Elvis has left us now".

The mourners rose to their feet and began to file past the coffin for one last lingering farewell to the man who had not just touched, but transformed, their lives. Last of all, Vernon Presley halted, bent over the casket and sobbed, "Oh sonny. . . just thank God there is a Lord."

The pall-bearers – Joe Esposito, Charlie Hodge, George Klein, Gene and Billy Smith, Jerry Schilling, Dr Nichopoulos, and Lamar Fike – lifted the casket shoulder-high and carried him on the first few steps of his final journey.

Through the doors of Graceland into the shadows cast by the towering colonnades, gleaming white in the sun. . . down the few stone steps and gently into a white hearse that stood second in a long line of white limousines. The trembling throng fell silent as they saw the casket. The day was still and quiet without even a breeze to rustle the leaves. Slowly the cortège moved off.

And then there was a crack like thunder. A young branch, still green, still bearing leaves, was ripped from a tree. It crashed to the ground, glancing off the limousine carrying Elvis's last girlfriend, Ginger Alden.

All along the boulevard people lined the route to the Forest Hill Cemetery. At the cemetery, the hushed crowd stood back and prayed with the family for a few short minutes before the casket was carried into the cool, white mausoleum to be laid to rest beside his beloved mother. Vernon emerged last of all, back into the sunlight, so weak, so frail, so drained, he leaned on his nurse and Joe Esposito for support. After the family left, the fans took their turn to file past the tomb, with only the sound of weeping disturbing an unnatural stillness.

In the 48 hours since Elvis had died the stock of every flower shop in Memphis and the surrounding area had been exhausted. New supplies were flown in from Colorado and California, and then even more. Now, in the shape of wreaths, guitars, teddy bears and crowns, they adorned the tomb of the King. By nightfall, when the cemetery at last closed its gates, not one flower was left.

Today they lie, pressed, still perfect, preserved for ever within the pages of a million books. Just as the music, the memory, the love of Elvis Presley lies, pressed, still perfect, preserved for ever within a million hearts.

Chapter Twelve

A
KING
FOREVER

◆

**By far the greatest memorial to Elvis is, without
doubt, the fidelity of his fans. Elvis Presley's
legacy is his music, his legend and the love he left
behind.**

It happens to all great men, but never in Life – Only ever in Death. It is as if mortality implies that what in life was marble is in death turned to clay. It was not long before the iconoclasts were chipping away at the feet.

Every aspect of Elvis Presley's life came under scrutiny or attack: his public life, his private life, his married life, his sex life. And even, would you believe, his afterlife. Everyone, it seemed, had a tale to tell, a story to sell. Most were friendly, harmless. Some were hurtful. One or two were even vicious. Elvis was no longer able to defend himself, and even if he had been, it is doubtful that he would have bothered. Like the British Royal Family he would not have given credence to rumour by rebuttal.

By far the most serious accusations made against Elvis were those that alleged misuse of drugs. It's often been said that Elvis was hopelessly hooked on what he called his "medication" – that he was a pill-popper, a junkie.

Most Elvis fans, however, refuse to accept that Elvis took drugs for any reason other than medical. Charlie Hodge, one of Elvis's favourite people, who lived at Graceland for nearly 20 years and was Elvis's right hand man on stage, is one of those fans. Charlie does not accept that Elvis took drugs for kicks. He remembers that during one show Elvis was unable to carry on. The Stamps were singing a gospel number in which Elvis played no part. Elvis whispered to Charlie, "I am almost exhausted." When the Stamps finished, Elvis called for his guitar and a stool. Then he sat at the edge of the stage, occasionally strummed a few chords and chatted to the audience about the early days in Memphis. For the audience it was something special. They loved it, and during this rest Elvis was able to summon enough strength to continue.

On another occasion Charlie recalls, in his book *Me 'n Elvis,* the heartfelt account of their friendship, how Elvis complained of "pain all over my body." It was known that Elvis suffered from various ailments for which drugs were legitimately prescribed, but much has been made of the stronger pills, such as Dilaudid, that are prescribed as pain-killers for people with cancer.

After Elvis died there was an autopsy which will remain a secret for at least another 40 years. Only Vernon Presley and the medical practitioners knew the full extent of what the autopsy revealed, but, shortly before he died, he was told by Elvis's personal

THE ELVIS DIARY

February 1978
The stage musical, Elvis, *opens in London to packed houses and wins the* Evening Standard *"Best Musical of the Year" award.*

16 August 1978
On the first anniversary of the King's death the Memphian Theatre shows a series of Presley films and memorial services are held for him in Memphis, attended by thousands of fans from all over the world.

1 September 1978
A 10-day convention "Always Elvis" is arranged by Colonel Parker at the Las Vegas Hilton. Again, thousands attend at which a bronze statue of the star is unveiled.

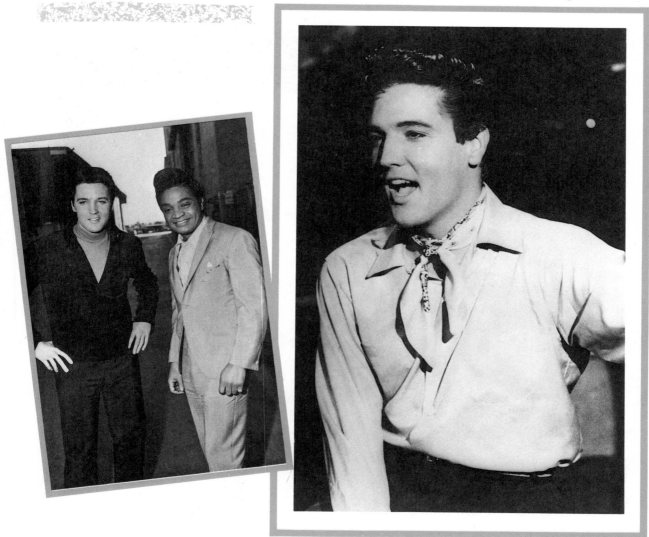

physician Dr George Nichopoulos, in the presence of Charlie, that the autopsy had revealed that Elvis had bone cancer that had spread throughout his body.

Towards the end of his life, Elvis's doctors must have known, or at least suspected, the true cause of his ill health. It is possible that even Elvis knew. It would account for many things: the rapid decline in his health and appearance, his intake of drugs, his obsessive determination to appear before as many of his fans as possible. The snipers had their day, but they never did win the day. They chipped away at what they hoped was clay and gave up when they discovered granite.

Elvis's death not only brought his critics out of hiding, it did the same for many of his fans. People who would never have called themselves Elvis fans or who had forgotten that they were Elvis fans, suddenly realized how much he had meant to their lives, the

LEFT: *Elvis with Jackie Wilson.*

RIGHT: *A favourite picture with the fans.*

OPPOSITE TOP:
Aloha From Hawaii.

OPPOSITE MIDDLE: ***Wild in the Country.***

OPPOSITE BELOW:
Viva Las Vegas.

RIGHT:
Wild In The Country.

BELOW: *Elvis with Priscilla and Lisa Marie.*

part he had played in their childhood, their romances, their marriages and their dreams.

From the moment he died, fans – and some speculators all over the globe – laid siege to record shops and newsagents, snatching up every last copy. Within hours of the announcement of his death, record shops everywhere were sold out of any Presley singles or albums. Within days, in Britain alone, nine Elvis numbers featured in the charts – including *Way Down* which went on to reach No. 1. In the United States six albums made the charts with Volumes 1 and 3 of Elvis's Golden Records reaching the top three. Even today his records are still selling in huge numbers with more and more regularly being certified Gold.

And it is not just his records. He has also inspired films about his life, as well as plays, musicals and documentaries. All over the world there are Elvis impersonators, ranging from kids who do it for kicks, to professionals who can command a million dollars a year working top Las Vegas venues.

Fan clubs sprang up throughout the world, and most of them still exist – the Elvis Presley Fan Club of Great Britain reputedly trebled its membership in the two years after his death.

In addition, a vast and lucrative market in memorabilia was tapped after his death. Anything that Elvis owned or even touched, from a Cadillac to a tube of squeezed toothpaste, has its value to his fans. Manufacturers, inspired first of all by Colonel Parker, soon started marketing Elvis keepsakes, ranging from wine, playing cards, sticks of rock, scarves, jackets, mirrors, ashtrays to jewel-studded dolls and grandfather clocks made from the trees of Graceland which sell for thousands of dollars. Even now, so many years after his death, this is a multi-million dollar market which shows no sign of decline.

On the day of Elvis's funeral 50,000 people visited the Forest Hill Cemetery and within months that figure had reached a million. Such was the strain on the cemetery's resources – and so great was the fear that the body would be stolen – that it was agreed that Elvis's body, along with that of his mother's, should be exhumed and reburied in the Meditation Gardens at Graceland.

In June 1982 Graceland was opened to the public. By the end of that year half a million people had visited the mansion. Even now a regular half-million people every year fly from all over the world to pay their respects of what has become a shrine to Elvis fans.

THE ELVIS DIARY

26 July 1979
Vernon Presley dies of heart failure.

17 August 1979
Tupelo, the town of Elvis's birth, opens the Elvis Presley Park and chapel – made possible by contributions from Elvis' countless fans and particularly Colonel Parker. The State of Mississippi declares Elvis's birthplace a Historical Monument.

16 August 1980
Memphis commemmorates Elvis by naming part of Beale Street (where Elvis gained his earliest musical inspirations) "Elvis Presley Plaza".

That's not all. Elvis's home town of Tupelo, Mississippi, has declared 8 January – Elvis's birthday – Elvis Presley Day. His adopted home of Memphis was a little slower off the mark, but, particularly with the election of Mayor Bill Morris, one of Elvis's greatest fans and oldest friends, that has now been remedied. Part of the legendary Beale Street has been renamed Elvis Presley Plaza and boasts a magnificent bronze statue, and Elvis Presley Boulevard, which runs past Graceland, must be the only major route in the world not to have signposts – ingenious fans keep thinking up ways of removing them even when they are placed 50 feet above the ground.

However, by far the greatest memorial, monument, tribute, to Elvis is without doubt the fidelity of his fans. Elvis Presley's legacy is his music, his legend and the love he left behind to be nurtured within the hearts of the International Family that is the Elvis world. Each and every one of his fans has a favourite record, photograph, film, memory and story. . . This is mine:

Elvis Presley commanded the stage; it was his domain. He was at the peak of his power as a performer. A colossus. A living legend. A King holding court, with his mesmerized subjects at his feet. From time to time he would reach over to Charlie Hodge and, with a twist of his wrist, take a silk scarf from the bundle draped around the guitarist's shoulders. Elvis would throw the length of silk carelessly around his neck as the screaming women at his feet became hysterical with hope and expectation. They knew that one of them, in just a few moments, would be the envied possessor of a piece of silk that had touched the very body of the King.

Elvis continued with his song, selecting the girl, giving time for the silk to become stained, just slightly, with his sweat. He noticed a young girl – no more than 12 – desperately trying to hold her place against the jostling of the bigger, older women. With an expert flick of his hand, Elvis directed the scarf into her outstretched, grateful arms.

He smiled as he witnessed her joy. She possessed a part of Elvis. For a moment. Just a moment. Then a hand reached out from the crowd around her and snatched the scarf away. Elvis saw the little girl's face crumple with grief, and he chopped the air.

THE ELVIS DIARY

8 January 1981
A resolution is introduced in the American Congress, Washington, to designate this date as "Elvis Presley Day".

3 April 1981
Warner Brothers' version of Elvis's life, This Is Elvis, *is released.*

27 September 1981
Life size Elvisly Yours bronze statue unveiled in London, England by Charlie Hodge.

THE REAL ELVIS

RCX 7190

THE REAL ELVIS

ELVIS PRESLEY

Side 1
DON'T BE CRUEL
I WANT YOU, I NEED YOU,
I LOVE YOU

Side 2
HOUND DOG
MY BABY LEFT ME

THE ELVIS DIARY

7 June 1982
Graceland is finally opened to the public.

14 May 1984
The million-dollar jet, Lisa Marie, is put on public display at Memphis Airport.

8 January 1985
The 50th anniversary of the King's birth.

The bewildered musicians came to an untidy halt mid-number. The audience was stunned into silence. The only sound was the heart-rending sobbing of the child.

Elvis moved to the edge of the stage and dropped down on one knee. He reached out and took the young girl's trembling hand. He gave it a little squeeze and let go. Then from around his neck he took the priceless gold chain and precious stone that he often wore on stage. Gently, so gently, careful not to mess her hair, Elvis placed the chain around her neck. He cupped her face in his hands and tenderly kissed her lips as he must often have kissed little Lisa Marie goodnight.

"There yuh go, honey, that's just for you", he said in a voice deep and husky from way down inside. He waved the security men to him. "You take good care of this lil girl, y'hear?" He took her chin in his hand, tilted her head, and gazed into the glazed, ecstatic eyes. Then he added softly: "Elvis Presley gave you that, honey. And ain't no-one can ever take that from you."

Today, around the world, Elvis fans are listening to his records, watching his films, staring at his portraits, feeling the warm, familiar glow of a tried and tested love. And they will be remembering the legacy of precious memories Elvis left in trust to each and every one of them.

They will savour all the pleasures and treasures that Elvis Presley's life gave them. . . the lasting friendships, the binding fraternity, the special moments and, of course, the music.

And perhaps this thought may cross their minds:

Elvis Presley gave me that.

And ain't no-one can ever take it from me.

By nightfall when the cemetery at last closed its gates, not one flower was left.

Today they lie pressed, still perfect, preserved forever within the pages of a million books. Just as the music, the memory and the love of Elvis Presley lies, pressed, still perfect, preserved forever within a million hearts.

ELVIS:THE FILMS

Love Me Tender (1956) Twentieth Century-Fox
Loving You (1957) Paramount Pictures
Jailhouse Rock (1957)
   Metro-Goldwyn-Mayer
King Creole (1958) Paramount Pictures
G.I. Blues (1960) Paramount Pictures
Flaming Star (1960) Twentieth Century-Fox
Wild In The Country (1961)
   Twentieth Century-Fox
Blue Hawaii (1961) Paramount Pictures
Follow That Dream (1962) United Artists
Kid Galahad (1962) United Artists
Girls! Girls! Girls! (1962) Paramount Pictures

It Happened At The World's Fair (1963)
   Metro-Goldwyn-Mayer
Fun In Acapulco (1963) Paramount Pictures
Kissin' Cousins (1964) Metro-Goldwyn-Mayer
Viva Las Vegas (1964) Metro-Goldwyn-Mayer
Roustabout (1964) Paramount Pictures
Girl Happy (1965) Metro-Goldwyn-Mayer
Tickle Me (1965) Allied Artists
Harum Scarum (1965) Metro-Goldwyn-Mayer
Paradise Hawaiian Style (1966)
   Paramount Pictures
Frankie and Johnny (1966) United Artists
Spinout (1966) Metro-Goldwyn-Mayer

LEFT: ***Viva Las Vegas.***

ABOVE: ***Roustabout.***

Easy Come, Easy Go (1967) Paramount Pictures
Double Trouble (1967) Metro-Goldwyn-Mayer
Clambake (1967) United Artists
Stay Away, Joe (1968) Metro-Goldwyn-Mayer
Speedway (1968) Metro-Goldwyn-Mayer
Live A Little, Love A Little (1968)
  Metro-Goldwyn-Mayer
Charro! (1969) National General Pictures
The Trouble With Girls (1969)
  Metro-Goldwyn-Mayer
Change Of Habit (1970) Universal Pictures
Elvis: That's The Way It Is (1970)
  Metro-Goldwyn-Mayer
Elvis On Tour (1973) Metro-Goldwyn-Mayer

Roustabout.

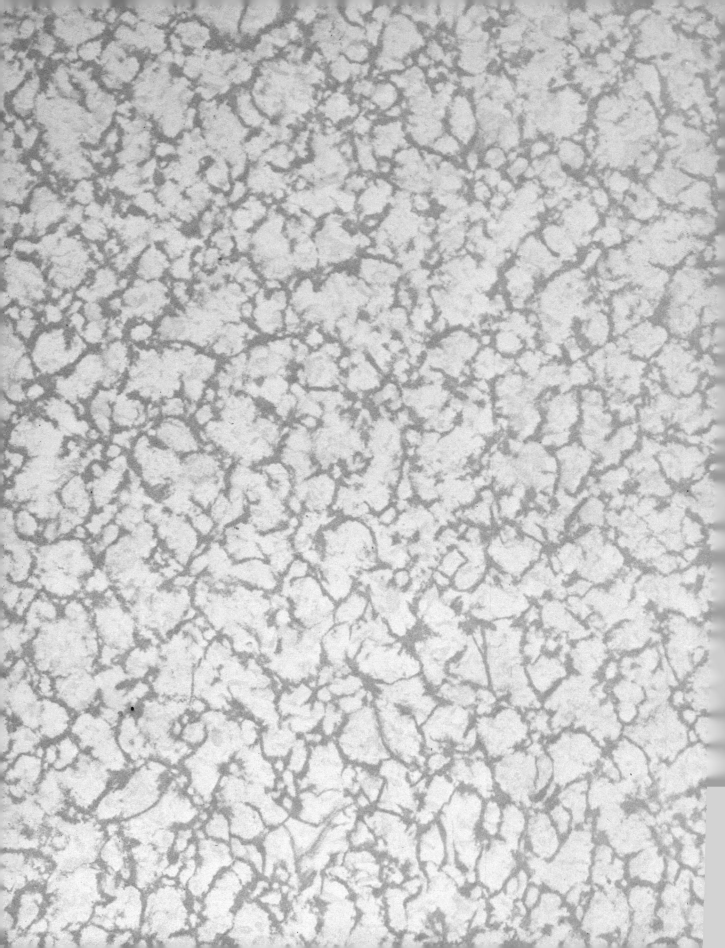